IS EQUAL OPPORTUNITY ENOUGH?

W9-CLL-072

made possible by a generous grant from
THE WILLIAM AND FLORA HEWLETT FOUNDATION

Editors-in-Chief Deborah Chasman & Joshua Cohen

Senior Editor Matt Lord

Digital Director Rosie Gillies

Audience Engagement Editor Ben Schacht

Manuscript and Production Editor Hannah Liberman

Assistant to the Publishers Irina Costache

Fellowship Coordinator Jasmine Parmley

Contributing Editors Adom Getachew, Lily Hu, Walter Johnson, Robin D. G. Kelley, Paul Pierson, & Becca Rothfeld

Contributing Arts Editors Ed Pavlić & Ivelisse Rodriguez

Black Voices in the Public Sphere Fellows Maya Jenkins & N'Kosi Oates

Editorial Assistants Cameron Avery & Zara Kulatunga

Finance Manager Anthony DeMusis III

Printer Sheridan PA

Board of Advisors Derek Schrier (Chair), Archon Fung, Deborah Fung, Richard M. Locke, Jeff Mayersohn, Scott Nielsen, Robert Pollin, Rob Reich, Hiram Samel, Kim Malone Scott, & Brandon M. Terry

Interior Graphic Design Zak Jensen & Alex Camlin

Cover Design Alex Camlin

Printed and bound in the United States.

Is Equal Opportunity Enough? is *Boston Review* issue 2023.2 (Forum 26 / 48.2 under former designation system).

Jo Guldi's essay is adapted with permission from The Long Land War: The Global Struggle for Occupancy Rights, *published in 2022 by Yale University Press.*

To become a member, visit
bostonreview.net/memberships/

For questions about donations and major gifts,
contact Irina Costache, irina@bostonreview.net

For questions about memberships, email
members@bostonreview.net

Boston Review
PO Box 390568
Cambridge, MA 02139

ISSN: 0734-2306 / ISBN: 978-1-946511-82-9

CONTENTS

ESSAYS

EDITORS' NOTE

Deborah Chasman & Joshua Cohen

EQUALITY OF OPPORTUNITY is a widely shared ideal. Across the ideological spectrum it is often held up as an economic model—a way of arranging access to education, work, and wealth—as well as a fundamental value, giving meaning to the notion that all citizens are equal. As Joe Biden put it in his first executive order as president, "equal opportunity is the bedrock of American democracy."

But is equal opportunity enough? Philosopher Christine Sypnowich thinks not. Taking equality seriously, she argues in the lead essay of this issue's forum, means aiming to ensure that we all live equally flourishing lives, not merely that we have equal chances to do so. Alarmed by what she considers an excessive focus on opportunity—and with it, choice and personal responsibility—she calls for a "more generous, substantive, and far-reaching egalitarianism."

Respondents debate the meaning of equality, in theory and practice. Some, such as Gina Schouten and Martin O'Neill, defend a substantive interpretation of equal opportunity. Others propose concrete policies and consider the political stakes of a radical egalitarian agenda.

The essays in this issue take up similar themes. Christopher Newfield examines the neoliberal rollback of equality in education, while Timothy Weaver explains why efforts to combat neighborhood poverty with "opportunity zones"—tax breaks for private investment—are misguided. Jo Guldi and Kevin Donovan imagine more equitable ways of thinking about land and finance. Nearly sixty years after Lyndon Johnson's commencement address at Howard University, this work illustrates the enduring struggle for "equality as a fact and equality as a result."

FORUM

WHAT'S WRONG WITH EQUAL OPPORTUNITY

Christine Sypnowich

THE LAST DECADE has delivered increasingly bleak portraits of vast inequalities in income, wealth, health, and other measures of well-being in many rich capitalist countries, from the United States to the United Kingdom. What should we do about them?

One common response is to argue that inequalities are only a problem to the extent that they reflect unequal opportunities. Economist Jared Bernstein, a longtime advisor to Joe Biden who has now been nominated to head the White House Council of Economic Advisers, expressed this view clearly in 2014 when he stated, "Opportunity and mobility are the right things to be talking about. . . . We always have inequality, and in America we're not that upset about inequality of outcomes. But we are upset about inequality of opportunity." Accordingly, in his first executive order as president, Biden proclaimed that "equal opportunity is the bedrock of American democracy." For his part, British Labour leader Keir Starmer has stated his party's aim should be to "pull down obstacles that limit opportunities and talent." And Prime Minister Justin Trudeau has intoned that in Canada, where I live, "no matter who you are . . . you have every opportunity to live your life to its fullest potential."

These statements are typical. In much of the West the tendency is to see equality as a matter of fairly distributed opportunities and to view an interest in outcomes as unreasonable, naïve, or even authoritarian. A similar focus on equality of opportunity is evident in the dominant strain of political philosophy in the Anglo-American world, liberal egalitarianism. In short, the prevailing political common sense tends to converge on the assumption that our egalitarian aspirations are realized once we have ensured equality of opportunity.

I think this view is seriously mistaken. Opportunity talk—and a host of ideas associated with it, including flawed conceptions of freedom, choice, and personal responsibility—plays far too central a role in our discussions of equality, poorly serving the egalitarian ideal and leaving a lot of inequality untouched. An egalitarian society should not shy away from a concern with outcomes, I will argue. Its goal must be that people live equally flourishing lives, not merely that they have the opportunity to do so.

The concept of flourishing, prominent in the socialist tradition, directs us to a more generous, substantive, and far-reaching egalitarianism. We care about inequality, this perspective stresses, because of its effects on people—not, or not only, because it violates an abstract principle of justice—and we lose interest in problems of inequality if the putatively unequal are doing equally well in their quality of life. Amartya Sen asked the classic question "equality of what?"—what is it, exactly, that egalitarians seek to equalize? The answer is flourishing, since whatever policies or principles we adopt, it is flourishing that we hope will be made more equal as a result of our endeavors.

At a moment of broad awareness of grave inequalities in our societies and eagerness to do something about it, it is essential to recognize that equality requires a focus on outcomes, not mere opportunities.

THE IDEA of equality of opportunity has played an important though complex role in progressive thought. As British historian Ben Jackson has noted, the notion "has a consensual and uncontroversial connotation" yet it is also "an exceptionally malleable concept, susceptible to an extraordinary range of interpretations." The radical left has often harbored an antipathy to the idea, viewing it as empty rhetoric in the face of persisting class inequality. Liberalism, by contrast, has long been dominated by a focus on equality of opportunity, though its meaning has evolved over time.

On one interpretation, the idea simply means that social barriers—racism or sexism, for example—should be eliminated in the competition for scarce and desirable positions. This is the meaning of equal opportunity instantiated in charters of rights that outlaw discrimination by the state and in a range of human rights policies that prohibit discrimination on the part of employers, landlords, and colleagues. From this perspective, the paradigmatic expression of equality of opportunity is something like the U.S. Civil Rights Act of 1964. Hence the well-known American expression "we are an equal opportunity employer."

As many have argued, however, opportunity has not truly been equalized simply because discrimination is outlawed at the point of housing or employment. Thus British socialist R. H. Tawney wrote in *Equality* (1931) that what is needed is not just "an open road" but also "an equal start." U.S. President Lyndon Johnson made a similar point at his 1965 commencement address at Howard University. "You do not take a person who, for years, has been hobbled by chains and liberate him, bring him up to the starting line of a race and then say, 'you are free to compete with all the others,' and still justly believe that you have been completely fair," he said. "It is not enough just to open the gates of opportunity. All our citizens must have the ability to walk through those gates." A year later, reflecting on the passage of major civil rights bills, Martin Luther King, Jr., called this next stage of struggle the "last steep ascent" of the civil rights movement. "The prohibition of barbaric behavior," he wrote, "while beneficial to the victim, does not constitute the attainment of equality."

These objections center on the idea that equal opportunity demands much more than the outlawing of discrimination and equal treatment before the law. It also requires far-reaching social and economic policy to transform unequal education and employment, which shape opportunity over the course of one's life.

The liberal egalitarian political philosophy that has prevailed in the West since the 1970s has taken this point seriously, as evidenced in ideas like John Rawls's notion of fair equality of opportunity, Ronald Dworkin's framework of equality of resources, and Sen's and Martha Nussbaum's theory of equal capabilities. Rawls, for example, contends that to ensure that talent is the only criterion for public offices and social positions, everyone should have a "fair chance." Achieving fair equality of opportunity, he argues, requires the elimination, or at least mitigation, of a host of barriers, including relations of domination, the influences of family income, and the impact of one's social class. Likewise, Dworkin's liberal egalitarianism models equality of opportunity on an insurance system for mitigating the effects of unjust inequalities.

These more substantial interpretations of equal opportunity have proven very influential. But it is noteworthy that they are quite compatible with significant inequality: just as the ordinary connotation of "opportunity" might suggest, some will fare better than others. Indeed, liberal egalitarians do not even aim for equality per se. Rawls accepts some inequalities so long as they benefit the worst off: this is the point of his "difference principle." Similarly, Dworkin takes for granted that there will be inequalities in a fully realized system of equality of opportunity.

Liberals contend that a focus on opportunity, rather than what opportunity achieves, has a host of advantages.

First, it is defended in terms of freedom. A focus on opportunity, the argument goes, respects individual freedom in making life choices. This follows from the principle of "neutrality" endorsed by Rawls and Dworkin, according to which the political community should not weigh in on what counts as a good life. There are rival views about how to live, and the state should not choose among them. As Jonathan Quong puts it, the neutral state is concerned not to treat citizens "as if they lack the ability to make effective choices about their own lives."

Second, a focus on opportunity is defended in terms of equality. Dworkin, for example, contends that an egalitarian principle justifies the mechanisms of the market. As Dworkin sees it, market exchange ensures that each person—their preferences and choices—counts for as much as any other, and the state is not able to betray any bias in favor of some plans of life over others. "A liberal theory of equality rules out . . . appeal to the inherent value of one theory of what is good in life," he writes. With its agnosticism about the good, the focus on opportunity is said to treat people with equal concern and respect.

Third, for many egalitarians, equality of opportunity means people can be held responsible for their choices. The state ensures that opportunities are equally available, and it's then up to individuals to take them up and live with the consequences.

Finally, equality of opportunity means that a truly meritocratic hierarchy can be achieved. This is valuable on grounds of fairness, the argument goes, since jobs, positions, and goods will go only to those who are qualified; it is also instrumentally valuable since society benefits from the best candidates being appointed to their relevant tasks. It is for this reason that Richard Arneson has characterized equal opportunity as "a political ideal that is opposed to caste hierarchy but not to hierarchy *per se*" because "the background assumption is that a society contains a hierarchy of more and less desirable, superior and inferior positions" that map on to people's capacities. This is made explicit in the egalitarian meritocracy of David Miller, for example, who defends the meritocratic ideal whereby "each person's chance to acquire positions of advantage and the rewards that go with them will depend entirely on his or her talent and effort."

Most liberal egalitarians are uneasy with inequality due to differences in talent, however, proposing that we distinguish between choice and circumstance. Dworkin offers a corrective to Rawls with the idea that a theory of justice should attend not to all inequalities, but only those due to a person's circumstances, be it their limited talents, tough family background, or the disadvantages that come with unanticipated bad luck. Inequalities due to "option luck"—that is, due to people's choices—are not owed compensation. People are responsible for their ambitions and tastes: it is down to them if they choose to gamble or squander their resources. If we respect the freedom to choose how to live, Dworkin contends, responsibility must be assigned to the individual for the mistakes she freely makes. On this view, a community may offer humanitarian assistance to those whose disadvantages are their own responsibility, but justice does not demand it.

With this focus on responsibility, what has been dubbed "luck egalitarianism" became a prominent and influential position among egalitarians. Luck egalitarians' hard line on responsibility suggests a sink-or-swim aspect inimical to the "to each according to his need" ideal of the socialist tradition. It may thus come as a surprise that luck egalitarianism garnered the endorsement of political philosophers on the left such as John Roemer and G. A. Cohen, who, earlier in their careers, were self-described "analytical Marxists." Roemer elaborated his own version of equality of opportunity that took account of the propensity of disadvantaged social groups to make poor choices, making the case that brute luck played a significant role as a cause of inequality. Nonetheless, the idea of responsibility reigned, and Cohen went so far as to salute Dworkin for performing for egalitarianism "the considerable service of incorporating within it the most powerful idea in the arsenal of the anti-egalitarian right: the idea of choice and responsibility."

On the luck egalitarian view, a hierarchy of rewards may persist under equality of opportunity, just so long as that hierarchy is not due to the social barriers of prejudice or family background, or even diversity of talent. On this "level playing field," inequality persists only because of individuals' decisions. Because it seeks to "correct for *all* unchosen disadvantages," Cohen contends, the luck egalitarian position can even be called "socialist" equality of opportunity. Shlomi Segall has made a more recent case for the relevance of outcomes, proposing a "non-responsibility" amendment to luck egalitarianism, which says that equal outcomes, however they emerge, are not unjust. Nonetheless, he defends the view that unequal outcomes are just if someone is worse off because it is "their fault." Even Elizabeth Anderson, one of luck egalitarianism's harshest critics, warns that a satisfactory alternative "heads off the thought that in an egalitarian society everyone somehow could have a right to receive goods without anyone having an obligation to produce them."

This prevailing emphasis on responsibility has proven to be very influential. Sen and Nussbaum reject liberals' narrow focus on economic goods, arguing that the impact of goods on capabilities is what matters—capabilities to be well-nourished, sheltered, or educated. But they too have tailored their view to take account of choice and responsibility. Capability theory takes quality of life—"what goods do" for people—as the appropriate egalitarian metric, but in practice, "respect for persons," as Nussbaum puts it, means deploying an opportunity-like measure: capability to function, not functioning per se.

Various attempts have been made to save the opportunity approach from the potential for harsh outcomes—for example, through social insurance schemes to protect people from the consequences of their bad choices. But they retain a laissez-faire aspect and fail to reckon seriously with how some people might fare quite badly. Opportunities are assured by a distribution of the means to whatever ends people seek to pursue, subject to their own responsibility for their choices, but after that, the political community steps back. In effect, the opportunity focus, in all its variants, washes its hands of how people are actually faring once it is determined that disparities in distributive outcomes are simply the result of people, as Arneson puts it, electing to "use and abuse" their equal opportunities. There may be humanitarian redress for disastrous outcomes in such cases, but egalitarian justice does not apply.

THERE ARE AT LEAST three reasons we should reject this focus on opportunity in egalitarian thought. Consider them in turn.

Choice as circumstance

IT IS DIFFICULT to draw a sharp line between what one chooses—in the sense of what one can be said to be responsible for—and what is the result of factors beyond a person's control. The question of responsibility enters murky waters of free will, determinism, and commonsense sociology about class divisions and social capital. But at least this much can be said: it is one thing to freely choose to do something, and it is another to be held responsible for the consequences, particularly if unjust social conditions incline us freely to choose badly. It is not just that the circumstance-choice distinction is hard to draw, especially since bad choices may result from economic disadvantage rather than the other way around. It also seems harsh to condemn the imprudent to impoverishment, particularly if their decisions are shaped by, and in turn reinforce, a class-divided society with lasting intergenerational effects.

The crude "talent plus effort" model of human endeavors thus looks like an unreasonable portrayal of how a human life goes, whatever weight one gives to either factor in the equation. Personhood is a dynamic process in which nurture and nature, circumstance and choice, are mutually constitutive. Individuals figuring out how to live—the appropriate next steps to take, what opportunities to avail themselves of—are mired in unjust social conditions that cannot be stripped away in order to isolate choice per se. Moreover, as Joseph Fishkin and Clare Chambers have noted, one choice can generate outcomes that themselves are not chosen and that further shape opportunities. For some, the path of life is largely how one door opens yet another. For others, all doors are closed, or, having closed one door, subsequent doors are not only closed to them but not even discernible; some doors immediately lock behind them; and some lead into rooms with no other exit. Inequality has a devastating effect on people's ability to determine the course of their lives. When people are in hopeless situations, in precarious work or chronically unemployed, in destructive relationships, suffering poor mental health, or living in dismal conditions, the odds of bettering one's lot look bleak.

In order to avoid a harsh approach to the consequences of choice, progressive luck egalitarians acknowledge that some disadvantages can result from choices so undermined by social factors beyond a person's control that they should be relegated to the domain of unchosen circumstances. In other words, instances of clear-cut, choice-induced lack of flourishing may be few and far between. After all, one cannot assume that imprudent persons are not contributing as best as they can—that is, as Marx put it, according to their ability, or as Cohen says, "appropriately" to their "capacity."

But if we go this route, ideas of luck seem beside the point, at best of mere polemical value in warding off right-wing challenges to the principle of redistribution. We put the cart before the horse if we attribute "bad luck" to outcomes we think of as unjust when encountering challenges deploying luck as a criterion for justice. As many critics have pointed out, from Anderson to Samuel Scheffler and Jonathan Wolff, better just to dispose of the unhelpful apparatus of luck egalitarianism altogether.

The greatest obstacle to embracing this conclusion may be the concern that doing so entails thinking of individuals as unable to control the direction of their lives. But this idea relies on a false understanding of the nature of agency, where individuals are freely choosing only if they are untouched by social influences. In truth, our desires, tastes, even needs, are shaped within a social context, molded by a myriad of influences. Liberals say that one's life goes better if led from "the inside," according to one's plans and goals. Certainly, a life cannot be lived any other way but from the "inside," but who one is "on the inside" is affected by her situation on the outside, the influence of a social milieu—including the damaging effects of social class and other ills endemic to capitalist societies.

In short, choices are never made in a vacuum: the tastes of friends, the values of parents and those with authority or influence, formative experiences in one's life, and superficial factors such as the symbolic value of a pursuit all contribute to what seems to us to be our choices about how to live. We must, as David Bakhurst puts it, "wean ourselves off the idea that the self is something purely inner and psychological." The personal is social and political—deeply shaped by "outer" factors, too.

Ignoring this does not spare us from social influence; it just defers to a certain kind of social influence—not just that of social class and other inequalities, but also, in particular, the influence of the market. Markets are often touted for conducting exchange according to the supposedly neutral measure of profitability, but market forces have significant consequences for the kinds of values one can pursue. The effects are often deleterious for human flourishing, even measured by people's expressions of satisfaction. And of course, market actors who influence our choices are not typically held to public account or democratic control.

If the individual is embedded in a complex weave of social factors, it is poor sociology to deem the ideal society as one where individuals enjoy absolute authority over judgments of value. And poor sociology makes for poor ethics, since refusing to exert political influence on the social environment leaves it open to all kinds of other influences, less worthy in their goals, and less transparent and democratic in their methods. The contrast should not be between individuals free to choose under a regime of neutrality as opposed to individuals rendered unfree by a focus on outcomes. Rather, what's at issue is how individuals' choices are constrained by an unaccountable market as opposed to individuals whose social environment is regulated by representative political institutions that facilitate good choices.

If by coercion we mean society rendering some choices more attractive than others, then a focus on flourishing is guilty as charged—but then so is just about any polity. Liberal societies today encourage some ways of life and discourage others: take state support for education and the arts, for example, and the lack of state support for, or discouragement of, harmful activities such as smoking. Indeed it is difficult to imagine any society not taking an interest in values and not justifying its policies by reference to them. The more pressing question is what methods a polity should deploy to enable citizens to live well. Out and out coercion, including punishment or threats to punish, should be inadmissible, but given that influence is inevitable, the responsible course is to embrace influence and to use it carefully, publicly, and transparently, guiding by incentives, education, and supporting institutions that offer pursuits of value.

Doing in order to be able to do

A SECOND REASON to reject opportunity talk is that it too easily concludes, in the face of unequal flourishing, that everyone has an equal opportunity to live a good life. It is difficult to truly attend to hindrances to flourishing simply by making choices available. If people fail to take up an opportunity and end up living unflourishing lives, the egalitarian attitude cannot be simply to acquiesce—to rationalize that the community did what it could, but people for their own reasons did not avail themselves of opportunities to flourish.

Rather, the egalitarian community will want to be proactive: to equip people to take opportunities through incentives and other social institutions, and thereby to encourage people to see the value of one choice over another, to appreciate why an opportunity is worthwhile. This may mean we need to introduce young people to pursuits that they are not inclined to take up, so that they are more likely to choose them. This does not mean forcing people to do anything, but it does mean taking unequal outcomes as a form of unjust inequality and seeking to intervene to enable people to make the most of their potential.

Often we need to do things in order to be able to do them. As Nussbaum notes, there are cases when "the absence of a function is really a sign that the capability itself has been surrendered." To ensure that opportunities will indeed be taken, we must engage in a substantive discussion about the value of various enterprises and eschew mere "cultural marketplace" conceptions of how people acquaint themselves with valuable options.

Now, this can all be turned into opportunity talk: that what is at issue is simply giving people genuine opportunities to flourish. But the flourishing view commits us to rather more effort than is historically associated with views that emphasize mere opportunity. And the enterprise is inherently outcome-oriented, insofar as it refuses to take people's choices—whether explicit or revealed—at face value and regards unequal outcomes as signaling the need for remedy. This means rejecting the neutralist paradigm in order to promote what is genuinely of value, to correct cultures of fatalism, low expectations, self-abnegation, or limited horizons. We should not be squeamish about an outcomes approach that takes a stand on how people should live.

Music is a good example of the kind of pursuit that may not be grasped as valuable or pursued over the course of one's life without some initiation into it in the first place. Even if we remove social barriers and equalize material resources, people will be differently situated and shaped by different social environments, which may disincline them to take up the opportunity to explore the arts. Ensuring universal access to music lessons, for example, is arguably not good enough. For flourishing to be equal, we need to develop incentives and social institutions that promote the valuable, and compulsory arts and music education, of the right kind, is arguably among them. Indeed, there is a sense in which mandatory education in pursuits not readily chosen can increase not just equality in flourishing but also our freedom—widening the choices available to a person, but also, as Charles Taylor has argued, ensuring that "what you want does not run against the grain of your basic purposes, or your self-realization."

Of course, in seeking to achieve equality of flourishing, we should take into account the plurality of ways of living well. Liberal egalitarians criticize outcome-focused views for weighing in on the meaning of "the good," with the implication that what counts as living well is narrowly understood. But an outcome-focused approach does not assume there are only a very small number of ways to live well, nor does it require that flourishing, in some form or another, be imposed by force. Flourishing comes in many forms, and judging that one form of life falls short, or does not warrant social support, need not unjustly restrict our freedom. The focus should be on identifying and supporting a range of paths to flourishing, even as we rule out promoting, or even opt to disincentivize, other forms of life.

These considerations also mean that the egalitarian society should seek to enable people to choose well, to become better choosers, to take responsibility. Contribution should not be a condition for the remedy of disadvantage, as on the luck egalitarian view. Rather, one's life goes better if one is contributing to the community, understood as broadly as possible, and not just in a narrow, productivist way. The flourishing picture understands failure to contribute as a source of disadvantage. Well-being involves taking an active part our communities if we are to live the life of "all-round development" extolled by Marx.

Nevertheless, we must be prepared to recognize persisting disparities in outcomes, not to acquiesce in them, but to propel us to revisit our policies—first, to ensure that they are truly the results of a diversity of valuable conceptions of how to live, and second, to open up the possibility that the options our society purports to make available, promote, and support, adequately capture what members of the community are properly interested in pursuing. After all, an egalitarian community must be prepared to revise what counts as valuable.

It is because flourishing matters that our egalitarian approach should allow for an element of maximization too. We cannot fall prey to the syndrome of leveling down, where we remove any additional measure of flourishing if it cannot be enjoyed equally by all. No amount of egalitarian social policy can fully negate the differences in disposition, health, or ability; after all, some of us cannot help but take a glum view on life. Nonetheless, we should be attentive to how inequality of outcome is the result of factors within our control. It is equal flourishing that matters, and we should not be hamstrung by a prohibition on seeking equality in how people actually live because of diversity about what counts as a good life.

Solidarity and outcomes

A THIRD REASON to reject opportunity talk is its sidelining of community. Despite all the discussion of responsibility among egalitarians, relatively little has been said about the responsibility members of an egalitarian society may have to their fellows, to enable them to be their equals. Marx, after all, despite his critique of capitalist exploitation as a "theft" of the worker's rightful product, ended up severing contribution from distribution in his communist principles. The principle of "from each according to his ability, to each according to his needs" connects the contributions and allocations of community members in a profound way. This is because in the egalitarian community the flourishing of others matters.

A focus on opportunity undermines egalitarian community with its excessive attention to individual choices and rewards in isolation from social connection. The ideal of solidarity and comradeship that has long been inherent in the egalitarian ideal means that members of a community care, or will come to care, about the flourishing of others. The community that radical egalitarianism presupposes requires that all see themselves as full participants with duties of mutual aid, or what Pablo Gilabert calls "solidaristic empowerment"—something that Cohen, for all his luck egalitarian inclinations, also underscored in his discussion of socialism and the idea of an "egalitarian ethos." Those who do well, be it a matter of effort or luck, are committed to sharing their benefits with others. Indeed, the lack of attention to the responsibilities of the lucky rich is a surprising feature of opportunity talk.

We are social beings insofar as our values are shaped by social circumstances, our well-being affected by our relationships, and our capacity to flourish in need of society's guidance and support. Dworkin makes the insightful point that inequality insults and diminishes the self-respect of citizens, the rich as well as the poor, but he does not say much about how that truth should shape the relationships of members of an egalitarian community. On the flourishing approach, our own flourishing is enhanced insofar as others are flourishing too. Socialist community involves relationships of trust, generosity, and fellow feeling, at odds with the grudging attitude suggested by luck egalitarians.

Indeed, the justice of much contemporary egalitarianism seems, as Wolff puts it, "soulless," sacrificing the relationships of solidarity that are usually thought to attend equality. The original egalitarian ideal of thinkers like Tawney involved harmonious relations where "to divide is not to take away," transcending "details of the counting house," not a society where, as Scheffler puts it, people make "heavily moralized judgments" about others' contributions. It seems a sad comment that arguments for equality today hearken less to Marx's communist ideal of a society where all have the means of life regardless of their contributions and more to Stalin's dictum that "those who do not work do not eat."

In short, the egalitarian community is committed to ensuring that people actually enjoy flourishing lives, and this is a social project. Liberal egalitarianism falls short as a truly egalitarian theory because its preoccupation with opportunity and freedom of choice leads it to forsake the relations of community at the heart of the equality ideal.

Stressing community has another important consequence: it can address non-material shortfalls in flourishing. This is not to suggest that material resources are not important for flourishing. Indeed, we should be skeptical of rival strands in egalitarianism that suggest that mutual respect or cultural recognition takes priority over, or can be separated from, people's material situation. On the contrary, shortfalls in respect or recognition are often, perhaps inevitably, deeply intertwined with material inequalities; facilitating equal respect, status, and power requires that we attend to unequal material resources.

But the truth is that flourishing has both material and non-material aspects. This was recognized by the Victorian thinker William Morris, whose aesthetic views prompted him to become a socialist, and who railed against how capitalism meant people's environments get "plainer, grimmer and barer" and how a "decent life" would involve "a beautiful world to live in," which he took to be an elaboration of Marx's egalitarian views.

People can also fail to flourish because they lack friendship or love—again, not always a matter of someone's material situation, and a problem we should expect to persist even if material conditions were equalized. Alienation and loneliness should be objects of egalitarian concern, but equality of opportunity puts them outside the scope of egalitarian justice. At a time when mental health is deteriorating around the globe, it is all the more urgent that our social policies devise ways to make people equal in well-being in a rich, substantive sense that enables rewarding relationships with others.

An emphasis on mere opportunity, preoccupied as it is with individuals making choices apart from the community in order to acquire the material means to unspecified ends, lacks the resources to challenge these significant sources of inequality. A focus on outcomes enables us to consider how people can be unequal in multifarious ways—often connected to their material situation, but sometimes not.

TAKEN TOGETHER, these considerations should undermine the preoccupation with opportunity in egalitarian thought. What is at stake in the pursuit of equality is human flourishing, and equal opportunities are insufficient insofar as they do not deliver equality in how people actually live.

What about the four benefits liberals attribute to a focus on opportunity? I hope to have shown either that these benefits are questionable or that an outcome approach can also, indeed better, provide them. First, a flourishing approach still respects individuals' freedom to choose insofar as it embraces a diversity of valuable options and pursuits. Second, it better serves equality by eschewing neutrality and acknowledging that different plans of life are in fact not equal and can produce radically unequal outcomes. Third, a flourishing life involves making valuable contributions to the community, so an outcome approach seeks to inculcate the virtues of responsibility. And finally, once we go further to inculcate support for valuable pursuits, the outcome approach nurtures people's talents more effectively, from which society might benefit.

These arguments are only the starting point for a political program focused on flourishing. Many questions remain. Guaranteeing equality of outcome is of course impossible; even the most benign human diversity will see to that. All the more reason that thought be given to what kinds of policies would advance equality in how people actually live, rather than what would simply expand opportunities. We also should consider how to facilitate legitimate, democratic debate about what counts as flourishing. In all this, however, it is essential to recognize that equality of opportunity is insufficient and that equal outcomes are in fact what we really care about.

Political philosophy's preoccupation with neutrality and personal responsibility have hampered a serious engagement with the pursuit of equality. Liberal egalitarianism has shed light on the injustice of economic and social disparities, but we need to be reminded of the truly radical implications of the egalitarian ideal. The realization of that ideal requires not just opportunities to flourish but actual flourishing, understood in all its manifold dimensions, from the material to the cultural and social. In short, the egalitarian ideal requires socialism.

EQUALITY OF RESULTS REVISITED
Leah Gordon

TROUBLED by growing inequality—as we all should be—Christine Sypnowich argues that opportunity-based egalitarianism is an insufficient tool for promoting a just society. I welcome her emphasis on equality of outcome, her focus on the non-material dimensions of flourishing, and her recognition that putting outcome-based egalitarianism into practice can be challenging because we all envision the good life differently. She effectively shows how far the landscape of liberal egalitarian thought has shifted toward opportunity-based egalitarianism over the last five decades.

In doing so, she joins a long debate over the meaning of President Lyndon Johnson's ambiguous injunction to seek "equality as a fact and equality as a result." This issue occupied many social scientists in the 1960s and 1970s. In thinking about how outcome-oriented egalitarian visions might be strengthened today, we should recall the pitfalls of these earlier arguments. In particular, outcome-oriented egalitarians must be explicit about the *causes* of unequal outcomes in order to avoid suggesting that cultural or biological factors—rather than unjust social and political arrangements—are to blame. Which results one is seeking to equalize—test scores, income, wealth, or other measures of flourishing—also matters enormously in generating the political will to translate egalitarian theory into practice.

On the first point, it is instructive to revisit the debate over sociologist James S. Coleman's influential report, *Equality of Educational Opportunity* (1966), which was commissioned under the Civil Rights Act of 1964. Despite its title, the report is notable for laying emphasis on outcomes; it spurred a new research paradigm that helped launch movements for educational testing and accountability. But both its findings and its methodology proved controversial. Based on statistical analysis of data from one of the largest national surveys of educational inequality produced by the mid-1960s, which surveyed 4,000 public schools and 645,000 students, the report found that factors such as increased school funding or per-student spending, improved facilities, and greater extracurricular offerings were not associated with better outcomes—test scores, in particular—for poor and minority students, though it did note that school desegregation by race and class was slightly correlated with smaller achievement gaps. "Whatever may be the combination of nonschool factors—poverty, community attitudes, low educational level of parents—which put minority children at a disadvantage in verbal and nonverbal skills when they enter the first grade," the report concluded, "the fact is the schools have not overcome it."

Many advocates of racial equality balked at this causal agnosticism, fearing that it opened the door to victim blaming. As I have detailed elsewhere, leading social scientific voices in the civil rights and Black Power movements—including Charles Hamilton, who coauthored *Black Power* with Stokely Carmichael in 1967—thought that Coleman's study, even if well intentioned, could backfire. Others worried that by exposing the persistence of unequal educational outcomes despite efforts to equalize educational inputs, such arguments could be used to blame African American families for achievement gaps, let racist school systems "off the hook," and rationalize reduced educational spending. This was no idle worry in the years when the Moynihan Report and Arthur Jensen's racist work alleging the largely genetic basis of intelligence were reasserting paradigms that "blamed the victim," in this case suggesting African American communities and culture—rather than structural and institutional racism—were responsible for intergenerational poverty.

Psychologist Kenneth Clark's *Dark Ghetto: Dilemmas of Social Power* (1965) helped explain how outcome talk, like opportunity talk, could obscure systemic discrimination. Clark would likely have agreed with Sypnowich that "it is difficult to draw a sharp line between what one chooses—and thus what one can be said to be responsible for—and what is the result of factors beyond a person's control." But in the educational context, this has meant that assigning responsibility for academic performance can be difficult—in the worst case, leading to mystification about the sources of unequal outcomes. Decrying a host of racist assumptions institutionalized in Harlem's white-led school system, Clark wrote:

> The fallacy in the assumptions does not mean that a system based upon them will be demonstrated to be ineffective; for once one organizes an educational system where children are placed in tracks or where certain judgements about their ability determine . . . how much they are taught . . . the horror is that the results seem to justify the assumption.

In pursuing equality of flourishing, we should be attentive to these risks of outcome-oriented advocacy that worried thoughtful critics in the past.

As for what types of results should be equalized, this too emerged as a focus of debate in the early 1970s. An influential study by a team of seven sociologists led by Christopher Jencks, *Inequality: A Reassessment of the Effect of Family and Schooling in America* (1972), emphasized that educational reform could not reduce economic inequality without a wider transformation of employment, tax, and welfare policies. "As long as egalitarians assume that public policy cannot contribute to economic equality directly but must proceed by ingenious manipulations of marginal institutions like the schools," the authors held, "progress will remain glacial."

This argument set off a firestorm of protest. Some social scientists accused Jencks of methodological errors. Many civil rights advocates took offense at the study's claims about race and heredity, and others argued that both Coleman and Jencks misread the political landscape. "Although Jencks's motives may have been meritorious," Ronald Edmonds and nine coauthors of "A Black Response to Christopher Jencks's *Inequality* and Certain Other Issues" (1973) argued, "in the effort to make his point about the need for fundamental social change his work does a disservice to black and low-income children." Since most liberals already knew that "it will take social change in addition to educational opportunity to right the wrongs of this country," Edmonds feared that *Inequality* would convince policymakers "that we need not worry about education because only social and economic change will bring about educational gain." And in fact, *Inequality* was published at a time of pervasive opposition to all types of educational equalization—right before *Milliken v. Bradley* (1974) undermined urban–suburban busing and *San Antonio v. Rodriguez* (1973) allowed states to avoid redistributive school finance reform.

To address these concerns, Sypnowich might clarify which outcomes progressives should try to equalize first. The trope of the "undeserving poor" has led Americans to be more generous in their educational than their social welfare policies, and the *Inequality* controversy illustrates the stark political obstacles to a policy agenda focused on equal socioeconomic—as opposed to educational—results. By removing merit "from the opportunity-results sequence," Donald Levine and Mary Jo Bane emphasized in 1975, calls to equalize economic results substitute "the notion that people should be rewarded according to their performance with the idea that worldly goods should be distributed more or less equally." And yet, by suggesting that "no individual really deserves anything," outcome-based egalitarian visions are "profoundly uncomfortable . . . for people living in a capitalist and ostensibly meritocratic society," since they imply that "the inequalities so long accepted as proper are, in fact, unjust."

I applaud Sypnowich for reviving attention to equality of results in a manner that is sensitive to the challenges of past efforts.

Gordon

Even so, since outcome-oriented egalitarianism competes with other deeply held American values—merit, private property, and a notion of family according to which one should be free to pass privilege to one's children—those of us who join Sypnowich in a pluralist, communitarian effort to promote equality of outcome should brace for a fight.

THE ART OF EQUALITY
William M. Paris

I WAS RECENTLY rereading Robin D. G. Kelley's magnificent book *Freedom Dreams: The Black Radical Imagination* (2002) when I came across his conclusion that "high expectations begot the civil rights movement." The movement's marches and sit-ins are often interpreted as struggles *for* equality: these men and women were fighting for a just society where their status as equals would be affirmed. On this view, equality—or at least a less unequal society—is an outcome to be established. But Kelley points out that equality is not only an end point for social progress; it is the spur of social action. In other words, equality is more than a status to be attained: it is a present *expectation*. To refashion Marx and Engels of *The German Ideology*, we might say that equality is not "a state of affairs to be established" but the "real movement" to transform the "present state of things."

Christine Sypnowich outlines various arguments philosophers have given in answer to the question "equality of what?" She argues, rightly in my opinion, that we ought to think of equality as equality of human flourishing rather than equality of opportunity. I agree wholeheartedly that we would do well "to be reminded of the truly radical implications of the egalitarian ideal." But I would like to shift the focus away from the ideal that offers us a standpoint from which to judge society and a goal that we can approximate. Equality is also fundamentally a matter of shaping the horizon of expectation for social relationships.

Equality is an intrinsically social concept: I can only be equal vis-à-vis others. Unlike freedom, which we can conceive of as a property of an individual, equality saturates the expectations we have of how we conduct ourselves with one another. A lone person on a deserted island may or may not be described as free, but they certainly could not have any expectations of equality. It is only within society that equality and inequality present themselves as problems. I would go further and say that the egalitarian ideal emerges from the real inequalities of social life.

Any movement to transform society begins from the sting of inequality. I could not feel anger at an instance of unequal treatment if I did not have the expectation of being treated as an equal. Without this expectation of equality, I may naturalize and rationalize unequal treatment as just. In *My Bondage and My Freedom* (1855), Frederick Douglass argues that the attainment of literacy irrevocably altered his expectations of how others ought to treat him. It is from the painful separation between how others treat me and the expectations I have of others that the egalitarian ideal acquires motivational force.

Kelley focuses on the importance of dreams because it is from the expectations drawn from a society that does not yet exist that we become the sort of people who can recognize the bitter sting of inequality. It might be thought that we do not need dreams to know when we are being treated unequally—that we respond spontaneously to treatment that violates our innate sense of dignity. But I think this response confuses the dignity we may have as human creatures with the active recognition that our dignity entitles us to certain expectations of how others may treat us. Our sense of dignity is historically and socially developed even if we allow for the idea that we naturally are equal creatures.

The development of our sense of dignity is a crucial component of the utopianism in the egalitarian ideal. I know very well that "utopianism" is usually an object of derision in both socialist and liberal discourses. Most philosophers and political theorists would rather burnish their "realistic" bona fides than be accused of vainly wishing for the impossible. Yet it strikes me that easy dismissals of utopia that reduce it to literary dreams of perfection radically misunderstand the motivational role of utopia in social life. Utopianism is not primarily about perfection but perfectibility; it expands our horizons of expectation for our social relationships. The radicality of the egalitarian ideal is that it reshapes and develops the ethical sense of our human relationships by giving us a glimpse of what should be.

In *The Principle of Hope* (1954), Marxist philosopher Ernst Bloch located this anticipatory potential—what he called *Vor-Schein*—in art. By producing a vision of a society with substantially modified social relationships, art estranges me from my current relations insofar as they no longer appear justifiable to me. The sweet dream of equality that I find in the dreamwork of art is only sweet because I come to recognize the bitter fruit I taste in daily life. Equality, I think, is as much a political state of affairs as an art to be cultivated.

Thus, my expectations of the norms of equality can be modified and reshaped. For instance, a society oriented around freedom of opportunity and individual responsibility can become desensitized to the declining life expectancy of its impoverished youth so long as it proceeds from their "free" choices of lifestyle. But if this state of affairs strikes us not only as unequal in fact, but also as a violation of the expectations we have of how society ought to be, then we may be moved to change it.

It is also conceivable that we can see evidence of inequality and think that the inequality is acceptable for either principled or pragmatic reasons. Such defenses reflect two different types of social expectations we might have. On the one hand, we might think that inequality is normatively justified, in which case it would be unjust to try to make society more equal. On the other hand, we might think that inequality is unjust but believe that attempts to alleviate inequality are either infeasible or will make life worse. But both of these attitudes—how I expect the world should be and how I expect the world to work—are expectations that can be shifted by the art of equality.

Defenders of social hierarchy, broadly construed, warn that certain appeals to equality contravene the "natural" order of things. They worry that egalitarian visions will inflate the expectations of the members of society and induce them to action. They are right to think that the expectations of equality are artificial rather than natural, but they are wrong to suppose that from this fact alone we ought to think that appeals to equality are less justifiable. My expectations of how others ought to comport themselves toward me are revisable—and necessarily so, since equality is not a fact but a social value.

Equality may be a utopian dream, but it is a real dream insofar as it alters the motivations of our actions. Learning how to take oneself as equal to others and what social commitments follow from taking oneself as equal are not given by nature. Socialist thinkers have not only been arguing for a more equal and flourishing state of affairs; they have been developing the very art of thinking equality. The strength of this art wanes when we lower our expectations. The strength and the promise of the egalitarian ideal is to raise our expectations and renew our reasons for acting.

Paris

THAT'S NOT SOCIALISM
Nicholas Vrousalis

I AGREE with Christine Sypnowich that equality of opportunity, even in its most radical forms, is insufficient for equal flourishing. But I do not think that equal flourishing is a good description of the egalitarian ideal. In particular, Sypnowich is mistaken in thinking that equal flourishing requires socialism and vice versa.

To kick off, does equal flourishing require socialism? Suppose that some enlightened capitalists get together with state officials to set up a system of equal flourishing. They commit their net profits to that end; they even appoint Sypnowich as chair of a Commission of Equal Flourishing to help them realize it. In this scenario—pure science fiction, but instructive nonetheless—we have equal flourishing, but subject to the decisions of a capitalist ruling class. In other words, we have equal flourishing without socialism, because socialism precludes class rule.

What about the converse—does socialism require equal flourishing? Sypnowich thinks it does, but this is also a mistake. In *The*

German Ideology Marx criticizes Max Stirner for advocating an infeasible and undesirable conception of self-realization: Marx's view is *not* "that each should do the work of Raphael," but rather "that anyone in whom there is a potential Raphael should be able to develop without hindrance." If this is correct, then equal flourishing is not part of the socialist ideal of equal freedom. To see why, suppose that Raphael and his twin are both unhindered in their pursuits of excellence. Unlike Raphael, his twin by choice fails to cultivate his talents and therefore fails to flourish, in any Sypnowich-consistent sense. I don't think there is anything to regret here. There is, by Sypnowich's definition, unequal flourishing, but there is no injustice. In other words, Marx's argument against Stirner also applies against Sypnowich: like Stirner, Sypnowich affirms a needlessly demanding account of socialist equality.

I think Sypnowich's discussion of liberal neutrality—the idea that justification for state policy cannot appeal to any conception of the good—also needs rethinking. Sypnowich is among the so-called "perfectionist" critics of this idea; she thinks neutrality is impossible. I agree with this claim and with the inference that Sypnowich draws from it: that a non-metaphysical, purely "political" liberalism is incoherent. But I disagree with Sypnowich's justification for rejecting neutrality. As I see it, neutrality does not fail because it allows undesirable *outcomes*, such as stifled lives, a soulless consumerism, and a concomitant mindless worship of the rich and powerful. Rather, these contemptible features of capitalist civilization stand condemned on the ground that they fail to reflect equal freedom.

This view is weakly perfectionist because it identifies equal freedom with the ability of individuals to set, pursue, and revise their plans of life independently of others. It is still perfectionist because it takes autonomy, summed up as the rational revisability of a life plan, to be good independently of whether anyone values it as good. But this form of perfectionism is still weaker than Sypnowich's substantive hierarchy of valuable *outcomes*—some excellent enough to count as flourishing, some not. On Sypnowich's view, equal freedom is defined in terms of successful outcomes. On my view, outcomes are irrelevant, unless inconsistent with the ability of each to set, pursue, and revise her ends independently of others. The upshot is that socialists differ from liberals in their theory of the right, not their theory of the good.

In the 1980s and '90s, Sypnowich's strong perfectionism seemed like a progressive idea. Many philosophers, from Charles Taylor to Michael Sandel, joined the perfectionist ranks in criticism of liberalism's allegedly "unencumbered" conception of the self, its putatively emaciated conception of choice, and its supposedly asocial characterization of society. But today we know that the so-called "liberal-communitarian debate" was worse than a waste of time. Time-wasting can, after all, be benign, whereas the communitarian position turned malignant. Not only did the communitarians fail to register any plausible criticism of liberalism; they also articulated "liberal nationalist" views readily co-optable by the populist right. Such inegalitarian political movements as British "Blue Labour," Flemish, Catalan, and Quebecois varieties of nationalism, as well as Trumpism and Brexit-style populism, found in communitarianism a rich repertoire of nativist ideas to draw from. Communitarianism itself eventually collapsed into various forms of nationalism, pure and simple.

Sypnowich is not a liberal nationalist, of course; her larger body of work attests to a consistent socialist internationalism. But her perfectionism vacillates. When asked "why contribute to *this* community, tradition, or culture?" Sypnowich's perfectionism is tempted by the communitarian answer—"because these traditions constitute authoritative horizons"—as opposed to the proceduralist answer: "because they serve everyone's equal freedom." But only the latter answer is immune to co-optation. This does not mean that unique cultures and traditions should be abandoned, but only that they should be supported if and only if such support is consistent with the equal freedom of all. This is also, I think, why the language of solidarity is preferable to the language of community. Under solidarity, you need only share a single cooperative end jointly with others. Under community, you need to share ends quite independently of their contribution to cooperation—this is what Sypnowich-style outcomes are all about.

Socialist internationalists should therefore reject a substantive perfectionism of outcome. They should jettison ideas like having an equal share in a "beautiful world"—perhaps a good slogan for the William Morris Furniture Coop, but not for a political program. And they should do so not just because beauty is subjective or essentially contested, but also because it is notoriously co-optable.

Instead, socialists should get busy elaborating the project of equal freedom that is close to Sypnowich's heart (and mine), namely of creating "an association, in which the free development of each is the condition for the free development of all." This concluding flourish of the second section of the *Communist Manifesto* represents an internationalist project that takes equal freedom as its premise and that discovers flourishing as a welcome byproduct of freedom's own exercise and self-justification. The reverse approach is undesirable and unnecessary to the socialist project Sypnowich exhorts us to undertake.

DESIGNING FOR OUTCOMES
John Roemer

CHRISTINE SYPNOWICH argues for a radical egalitarian ideal according to which people possess "not just opportunities to flourish but actual flourishing." In making her case, she attacks equal-opportunity theory—luck egalitarianism, in particular—for merely equalizing opportunities, which in her view won't guarantee radical egalitarian outcomes because poor outcomes will be attributed to poor choices.

Thus, Sypnowich is a left-wing critic of equal opportunity: she believes that it endorses unacceptably high levels of inequality and holds individuals responsible for too much. Indeed, she considers any talk of responsibility regarding opportunity as being ipso facto right wing.

Yet equal opportunity theory is itself neither left- nor right-wing; it prescribes a degree of redistribution, or compensation for disadvantage, that reflects our choices about the goal we are aiming for. The more circumstances—the social and biological facts that people are born with or into—that we correct for, the greater the benefit for the disadvantaged and the less individual responsibility will matter. As a quite radical egalitarian, I would choose a large set of circumstances, but equal opportunity theory is flexible. As I proposed in my 1993 model of equal opportunity theory (EOp), each society can choose the set of circumstances to address and set policy accordingly.

In EOp, we begin with a population and choose to maximize some objective—perhaps a narrow one, such as wage-earning capacity, or perhaps a more demanding and complex one, like flourishing. We say someone is advantaged if their circumstances are propitious for achieving that objective; otherwise we say they are disadvantaged. The goal of the state (or the equal-opportunity social planner) is to choose the policy—from set of feasible policies that the state can provide—that maximizes the average value of the objective for those who are most disadvantaged. The values of the objective will vary even among people with the same circumstances because of their individual choices, or effort. We call all individuals with the same circumstances members of the same *type*.

If the objective is wage-earning capacity, the policy might be a tax rule that collects funds to finance education. Typically, the tax policy collects funds from citizens and allocates them unequally: more disadvantaged children receive more educational resources. Say that a policy is *complete* if the average value of the objective is the same for advantaged and disadvantaged people alike. Complete policies are a rarity. Nonetheless, EOp policy can be said to "level the playing field" through social provision of resources to disadvantaged types. This concept of equal opportunity is different from a meritocratic approach, which seeks to correct only for discrimination.

In EOp theory, members of the population are viewed as not being responsible for their circumstances, but they are responsible for their efforts or choices to the extent that the model allows it. Some members of a disadvantaged type may make poor choices relative to the actions of others with the same circumstances. However, if being poor choosers is characteristic of people with certain circumstances, its members will be compensated, not punished.

On this model, the more conditions we categorize as circumstances, the less choice matters. As the grid of circumstances becomes ever finer, each individual will eventually be the sole member of their type. In this extreme case, circumstances determine everything, and equality of opportunity dissolves into equality of outcomes. If we choose a small set of circumstances, by contrast, choice (or effort) becomes very important; in the extreme, there is only one type, and individuals are fully responsible for everything. The more social democratic a society, the more circumstances it will use to justify compensatory social policy. When conservatives complain that the welfare state manages a person's life, they mean that leftist social planners annihilate the role of choice.

The model I have presented covers many possible situations, but I will not claim it can be applied to every problem. If it applies, then a society or planner, by their choice of circumstances and typology, can produce an equal opportunity policy that is consonant with its views on how free individuals are to affect the outcomes they come to experience. As G. A. Cohen writes in *Why Not Socialism?* (2009):

> Socialist equality of opportunity seeks to correct for *all* unchosen disadvantages, disadvantages, that is, for which the agent cannot be

held responsible, whether they be disadvantages that reflect social misfortune or disadvantages that reflect natural misfortune. When socialist equality of opportunity prevails, differences of outcome reflect nothing but difference of taste and choice, not differences of natural and social capacities and powers.

Sypnowich's goal would be to choose a social policy that equalizes the personal level of flourishing over all members of society, at the highest possible level. (Because this goal will be vulnerable to the leveling down objection—the thought that to make us equal, we should simply reduce the advantaged to the level of the most disadvantaged—she might instead take the goal as maximizing the minimum level of flourishing over all citizens.) Note that, for Sypnowich, circumstances and choice are irrelevant in defining the social optimum; how policies bring about distributions of flourishing is the only relevant factor. We cannot engage in responsibility talk in her model because it has no implications for what the social optimum is.

The EOp approach is different. As a social scientist, I try to keep an eye on the data. We want models that can be calibrated with available data sets. Philosophers often do not so constrain themselves. Using available data sets, one can run the model and calculate actual social policies that equalize opportunities, as a function of the set of circumstances we choose to represent our views on what individuals should be held responsible for.

There is an ever-growing statistical literature that employs data to calculate how much inequality in different countries is due to inequality of opportunity. That is, one can decompose total inequality—of income, for instance—into parts due to differential circumstances and differential effort or choice. Only a few rich countries have data sets that collect information for a sufficiently dense set of circumstances. For the United States, using the most complete data set, we estimate that about half of income inequality is due to circumstances, and the other half is due to the effort and luck. This surely underestimates the true role of circumstances, as there are doubtless circumstances we do not record. But we can still use the EOp theory to advocate equality-increasing reforms.

For any social planner, the question remains of how to treat children in a responsibility-sensitive model. In my view, children up to an age of moral consent should not be held responsible for anything that they do. (This does not apply to how we teach children social behavior.) Below the age of sixteen, say, data about a person's accomplishments and behavior should be viewed as a circumstance. Thus, the biography of the child up to the age of sixteen would be described as a set of circumstances; both nature and nurture are circumstances. With this in mind, the EOp model will advocate large expenditures on children under sixteen and quite radical reforms in education.

In short: despite Sypnowich's skepticism, the EOp approach can be an effective strategy for equality of outcomes, as it calculates a policy that can equalize outcomes to a chosen degree. We only need to agree on our goal.

Roemer

USE WITH EXTREME CAUTION
Ravi Kanbur

I WELCOME Christine Sypnowich's powerful corrective to the ongoing drift in egalitarian circles toward opportunities and away from outcomes. I have argued in my own writings as an economist that this drift is not merited on conceptual, empirical, and policy grounds. Consider each domain in turn.

Concepts

THE OPPORTUNITY ARGUMENT is that while outcomes that flow from factors outside the control of individuals are legitimate targets for correction, outcomes over which individuals have had choice and control do not warrant such correction. But the distinction faces conceptual problems right from the start.

Sypnowich rightly highlights the difficulty of drawing a line between circumstance and choice. We should consider as well the many cases where one person's choice becomes another person's circumstance: think of parents and children, teachers and pupils, or corporation executives and their workers. Moreover, think of the myriad choices in markets that shape outcomes for individuals at large. Free choices by high-income individuals in the property market push up property values and rents and push out low-income tenants; the *circumstance* many renters face is caused by the free *choices* of high earners. And as Sypnowich argues, it is furthermore poor sociology to ignore the influences of community and society—and "poor sociology makes for poor ethics."

Sypnowich touches briefly on the opportunity dimension of the capability approach developed by Martha Nussbaum and Amartya Sen. I agree with her comments; elsewhere I have presented a detailed critique of the capability approach, lauding its "broadening of the evaluation space from the instrumental means such as income to the intrinsic ends of beings and doings, or functionings" but strongly cautioning against "the further broadening of evaluation from achievement of ends to opportunity to achieve those ends—from functionings to capabilities." At a normative level, it is essential that ends be valued in themselves.

Empirics

OVER THE LAST TWO DECADES there has been an explosion in attempts to quantify "inequality of opportunity," particularly for developing countries. The exercise took off after the World Bank embraced the effort in its 2006 *World Development Report*, "Equity and Development."

Though this work continues to advance in econometric sophistication, the procedure is quite straightforward at its heart. First, identify a set of circumstance variables. In an influential early study by Paes de Barros and colleagues on Latin America and the Caribbean, these were selected as gender, race/ethnicity, birthplace, mother's education, father's education, and father's occupation. (Note how few variables make the cut!) Second, identify an outcome variable: say, income. Third, quantify the fraction of variation in the outcome variable that is accounted for by the circumstance variables and their intersections—and call this "inequality of opportunity." In the Barros study, the numbers turn out to be of the order of 20 to 50 percent; recent reviews put the range at 10 to 60 percent across countries.

This method faces many obstacles and limitations. For cross-country comparisons or assessments over time, the circumstance variables need to be comparable. If data on the level of father's education is given in ten categories in one country and five categories in another, the ten categories have to be aggregated to match the five. Similarly, if a circumstance variable of interest is totally missing from a country's data source, the calculation for that country is not comparable to other countries. And data on many circumstance variables of interest simply does not exist.

As a result, we are effectively driven to the lowest common denominator of empirical information, leading to the coarsest possible picture. The smaller the number of variables, the lower will be the overall variation accounted for by these variables—and thus the lower will be the measured inequality of opportunity we present to the world and to policymakers! One defense that is often mounted is that this measure can and should be presented as a lower bound: inequality of opportunity is "at least" 30 percent, we might say. But without an upper bound, technically we could not be contradicted in saying that the number may be as high as 70 percent, 80 percent, or even 100 percent. It is disconcerting that such an important calculation should be so dependent on mundane properties of the data.

In another major strand of empirical work, the Human Development Report's Human Development Index (HDI) and its Multidimensional Poverty Index (MPI) are both explicitly modeled on the capability perspective. But in fact they are largely based on achievements, not opportunity for achievements. At the national level, for example, the HDI is a weighted sum of per capita income, years of schooling, and life expectancy. The broadening from a sole focus on income is certainly welcome, but years of schooling is a measure of a functioning, not capability or opportunity for schooling; the same goes for life expectancy. (Of course, schooling—and life itself—also provide opportunities for other kinds of functionings, but we are back to a conceptual difficulty or normative debate: Why should we think of education or life expectancy solely as opportunities for functioning, instead of as outcomes valuable in themselves?)

It is indeed difficult to see how we could go beyond functionings with the available data. The same is true of the ten components of the MPI—as its originators have admitted. In practice, then, we are back to measuring variation in outcomes.

Policy

IN POLICY CIRCLES, opportunity arguments are often couched in terms of "pre-distribution" being superior to "redistribution." A standard formulation says that it is better to provide equal public education (pre-distribution) and then let the chips fall where they may through effort and choice rather than have a progressive tax regime that takes income from some and gives it to others or invests in public goods (redistribution). But again, it is difficult to separate pre-distribution from redistribution, especially when parental inputs combine with publicly provided education to determine quality of education and its market outcomes.

The idea of pre-distribution is also present in the work of those such as Raj Chetty and colleagues who propose targeted fixes to get people out of areas where intergenerational mobility is low. But as with education, two issues arise. First, the resources needed for pre-distribution will have to come from taxation, which raises the question of how progressive the taxation should be. Second, as Dylan Matthews notes in *Vox*, the fixes do not "dismantle the structural causes of segregation, or prevent rich families from using their political power to keep out poor families."

It is sometimes argued that equal opportunity talk is more palatable in policy circles than talk of equalizing outcomes—so egalitarians should embrace the former if they want a seat at the table. But if this is the price of admission, egalitarians may find themselves boxed into limits on policies like substantial redistribution and progressive taxation. Moreover, saying things like "inequality of

opportunity accounts for at least 30 percent of observed inequality"
is likely to prompt a dismissive eye roll from policymakers: "But that
means equality of opportunity could be 70 percent, which is not at all
bad, and I have many other things to worry about." At a minimum,
economists with egalitarian commitments should embrace freedom
from poverty as an essential corrective to equality of opportunity.

Putting all these considerations together, I would rather that
there was a strong health warning for egalitarians who are drawn to
equality of opportunity: "Use with extreme caution!"

BEYOND CHOICE
Anne Phillips

I ENTIRELY AGREE with Christine Sypnowich that equal opportunity is not enough. Focusing on opportunity prioritizes choice over equality. It washes its hands of how people end up so long as their situation can be half-plausibly attributed to the exercise of choice in conditions of roughly equal opportunity. The attribution is never fully plausible, given the difficulties regarding what counts as free choice, and the equality is always rough. The resulting acquiescence in what can be a startling inequality of outcome betrays the solidarity and comradeship that ought to characterize an egalitarian community.

This is strong language in a world more accustomed to thinking of equal opportunity as the acceptable face of equality, immeasurably superior to its demon other: equality of outcome. To be fair, the concept of equality of opportunity does do some useful work, providing arguments for greater educational equality, against discriminatory employment practices, and—though rarely followed through—in favor of high levels of inheritance taxation so as to limit the cascading of privilege across generations. But this familiar account of equality of *opportunity*, laying stress more on the latter word than the former, already reveals the only mildly ameliorative objectives usually attached to the phrase. This is nothing like *equality* of opportunity: that would involve something far more robust than greater educational equality or higher levels of inheritance tax. And even if we were to move more firmly in that direction, equality of opportunity largely directs attention to our starting points, taking it for granted that we are competing for a limited number of favorable and better-rewarded positions, and accepting that only some of us can succeed. The function of equality of opportunity is in many ways ideological, diverting us from wider ambitions and encouraging us to believe—against all credibility—that the inequalities that characterize the contemporary world, both domestic and global, reflect what each of us has made of our opportunities.

Where I differ from Sypnowich is on the point she undoubtedly sees as most important to her argument. The real target of her critique is those who complacently accept the choices people make as authentic exercises of their freedom, who are blind to the ways choices are shaped by institutions and markets, and who regard any attempt to shape them in a different or more positive direction as illegitimate interference. Thus she "refuses to take people's choices—whether explicit or revealed—at face value" and argues for active promotion of the kind of choices or pursuits that would better enable human flourishing—and would lead, therefore, to greater equality of outcome.

Some of this is unexceptional. I am not particularly at odds with Sypnowich's skepticism about taking choices at face value. She is not suggesting that there is only one kind of flourishing, nor is she proposing coercive or punitive mechanisms to get people to make what are deemed better choices. And anyone who has lamented the narrowing of horizons in contemporary schooling would cheer her on when she argues that an egalitarian community would introduce young people to pursuits they are not initially inclined to take up—exposing every child to music, for example, or to activities they do not yet like in order to discover whether they do.

But despite its critique of liberal egalitarianism's excessive focus on choice, Sypnowich's argument itself remains very much within the choice framework, accepting that how we fare is indeed an effect of the choices we make. It challenges only the tendency to treat those choices as self-standing and insulate them from either community or government interference.

The resulting focus on what would make us "better choosers" obscures the structural character of inequality. It also significantly understates the vastness of current inequalities in income, wealth, health, and well-being. We do, of course, make good and bad choices in our lives, and the mess we sometimes end up in can often be traced back to previous bad decisions. But for the majority of us, what we do or do not choose has only a marginal effect on how fully we flourish; most of that is already set in train by where we started from and what grudging opportunities our society currently has to offer. When we understate the structural nature of this inequality, we understate the scale of the egalitarian challenge.

We also inadvertently collude in the alibis that governments have found all too convenient when pressuring people into activities that are far from beneficial to a flourishing life. The United States and the United Kingdom currently have the most punitive welfare-to-work regimes in the world, making access to welfare benefits, including for those caring for very young children, conditional on seeking out whatever work is currently available—regardless of how irregular the hours, how poorly it is paid, or how little it uses existing skills. This is justified again and again in the language of incentivizing people to make the "better" choice of work over idleness, independence over dependence, with no acknowledgment that those pressured into the lowest reaches of the labor market are likely to remain trapped there for the rest of their working lives. This is not in any way what Sypnowich has in mind: she has no time for the punitive incentivizing that threatens to remove welfare benefits from people who fail to make the "right" choice. But in focusing so heavily on what encourages bad choices and what would enable better ones, she remains too much within a framework that explains bad outcomes by reference to bad choice.

In endorsing the idea that societies should "inculcate support for valuable pursuits," Sypnowich also leaves hanging some troubling questions about who determines what counts as valuable. Like her, I am no great defender of neutrality, but we live in a world marked by vast differences in status as well as by material inequality, with pervasive disparagement of those regarded as lesser on account of their social class, race, or gender, and much easy dismissal of the views of those considered less educated or articulate. Against this background, the language of "better choice" or "more valuable pursuits" carries hostages to fortune, and these are hardly dispelled by a brief reference to facilitating legitimate democratic debate about what counts as flourishing.

In most cases, indeed, those who are not flourishing have a very clear idea of what would make their lives go better, and this typically involves insisting on their equal status as full members of society—think, for example, of Black Lives Matter—and claiming a greater share of society's material resources to make that equality meaningful. The chances of shifting outcomes in the more egalitarian direction favored by Sypnowich will depend far more on the resistance of those currently stuck with poorer outcomes, and their ability to challenge the powerful forces ranged against them, than on the nudging of presumptively well-intentioned governments.

THE RADICALISM OF EQUAL OPPORTUNITY
Martin O'Neill

CHRISTINE SYPNOWICH presents several telling criticisms of some recent trends in thinking about social justice within liberal political theory. I agree that a one-eyed and exclusive focus on equality of opportunity can lead to a distorted and impoverished viewpoint that loses touch with the real core of equality. But I am unconvinced that all or even most liberal egalitarian views fall within the purview of her criticisms, and I think that she greatly underestimates the radical potential of liberal egalitarianism as a philosophical tradition—and in particular, of the frequently undervalued Rawlsian idea of fair equality of opportunity.

Sypnowich's arguments are very effective against *luck egalitarian* views, which put questionable conceptions of choice and responsibility at the center of a rather narrow and moralistic conception of distributive justice. But these criticisms do not apply to her broader targets; Rawls, for example, was not a luck egalitarian avant la lettre. Sypnowich is too quick to tar liberal egalitarians in general with the brush used against luck egalitarians in particular.

Take the claim that "liberal egalitarianism falls short of a truly egalitarian theory because its preoccupation with opportunity and freedom of choice leads it to forsake the relations of community at the heart of the equality ideal." This criticism hits home only against a dwindling minority of liberal egalitarian views: those developed in the 1980s in the wake of Ronald Dworkin's account of "equality of resources." In two highly influential articles both published in 1989, G. A. Cohen and Richard Arneson presented closely related versions of luck egalitarianism that, starting from Dworkin's position, developed a starker and simpler view that aimed to put the distinction between choice and circumstance at the center of egalitarian thinking. Both emphasized individual responsibility as a kind of obverse complement to egalitarian concerns, marking out a territory of individual freedom that egalitarians should seek to protect, and looking to create a kind of zone of individual consequences with which egalitarian policy interventions should avoid intervening. Cohen called his view "equality of access to advantage," while Arneson called his "equality of opportunity for welfare," but their differences were dwarfed by their similarities.

Luck egalitarianism was philosophically influential, at least initially, in part because its emphasis on the connection of distributive justice to ideas of choice, responsibility, and individual freedom created philosophical puzzles of considerable interest and complexity. But this view has been in abeyance, at least among political philosophers, during the last quarter century. Among those whose work has helped to save liberal egalitarianism from the cul-de-sac of luck egalitarianism—and who have sought to deepen the public discussion of equality, in part through the pages of this magazine—are T. M. Scanlon, Elizabeth Anderson, Samuel Scheffler, Debra Satz, Stuart White, and Joshua Cohen. As a result, the leading philosophical versions of liberal egalitarianism today are quite different: so-called "social" or "relational" egalitarians view equality as a matter, first and foremost, of relating to each other *as equals*, not as an arithmetical matter of achieving—or setting up equal opportunities to achieve—an equal level of material resources, welfare, or some other distributive metric. Social egalitarian ideas can stand behind an ambitious form of liberal egalitarianism that might endorse, for example, the socialized provision of child care and lifelong education, or policies of local economic development that look to expand the cooperative sector and democratize the economy.

Does this mean that we should throw out equality of opportunity along with luck egalitarianism? Far from it. When given an appropriate scope and role (rather than taken to constitute a complete account of the demands of justice), the idea is attractive, combining an uncontroversial outward appearance with a surprising degree of hidden radicalism.

Take Rawls's idea of fair equality of opportunity (FEO), which is the first part of Rawls's second principle of justice. (The second part is his much better known—and more widely discussed—"difference principle.") According to FEO, access to different jobs and to positions of power and responsibility within the economy should be distributed in a way that, to the extent institutionally possible, eradicates the influence of background social conditions. A society that realizes FEO is one that strives through a broad range of fiscal and social policies to ensure that the likelihood that any individual occupies any particular job or social position—from the most powerful and prestigious to the least—should be entirely divorced from their race, gender, sexual orientation, and social and family background. When we endorse FEO, we are endorsing a commitment that amounts to nothing less than the idea of the abolition of social class, at least when seen as a feature that structures life chances from one generation to the next. This is hardly a minimalist commitment, and it gives a standard for assessing economic justice that contemporary societies such as the United States and the United Kingdom, for example, conspicuously fail to meet.

Sypnowich acknowledges that FEO goes well beyond mere nondiscrimination, yet she nevertheless portrays it as far too complacent regarding actually existing inequality. This seems to me a mistake, especially when one thinks about the kinds of policies that would be justified by FEO. Given that unequal material outcomes in one generation can translate into unfair opportunities in the next generation, the ideal of equal opportunity is far from weak or inert. Rawls himself endorsed aggressive forms of inheritance taxation and capital transfer taxation as one way to make sure that unfair inequalities of opportunity were not transferred from one generation to the next. (This was one important element of his idea of a "property-owning democracy.") For related reasons, Rawls also advocated designing an educational system that actively counteracts existing social inequalities. Such an approach would take us very far from the existing realities of U.S. and U.K. education systems and toward the well-funded, universalist, and egalitarian systems in countries such as Finland. In short, taking FEO seriously means embracing a transformative egalitarian agenda that touches upon a wide range of policy areas.

For Rawls, of course, FEO was only one element of a richer and more complex account of the demands of justice; other views of the role of equal opportunity within liberal egalitarianism are possible. Sypnowich's socialist egalitarianism may have other grounds for rejecting its liberal counterpart, but it should not be too quick to downplay the power of equal opportunity, or to miss out on the potential of liberal egalitarianism as a broader body of thought to advance compelling justifications for institutions and policies that radical egalitarians should find politically attractive.

NO EQUALITY WITHOUT LIBERAL EQUALITY
Zofia Stemplowska

PEOPLE ARE UNEQUAL in endless ways. They are rich and poor. They belong to different genders, ethnic groups, and states. Some have or want to have children; others don't. No one who is advocating for egalitarian justice argues for equality in all possible respects. But which of the differences matter?

Social egalitarians argue that equality requires people to enjoy equal social status: no one can be anyone else's social inferior. On the most prominent social egalitarian view, inequalities in other goods matter only insofar as they bear on equality of social status. I am not a social egalitarian of this type because I think that social equality matters but it is not the only equality that matters. Social equality on its own is compatible with too many inequalities in the goods that people care about. People who are born not too well off or who lack access to fertility treatments, for example, may still enjoy equal social status, but they lack equality in other important ways. Perhaps social egalitarians can explain how those inequalities are incompatible with equal social status. But even if they did, those inequalities are objectionable not only when and because they bear on a person's social standing. They are objectionable because people's lives can go better or worse in ways unrelated to their social status.

Egalitarian views that care about inequalities beyond those of social status are sometimes called distributively egalitarian. I assume that the equality of flourishing view that Christine Sypnowich puts forward is a distributively egalitarian view. But, like Marx, Sypnowich offers a case for the system she prefers by focusing on criticizing the alternative, so we learn little of what her preferred view entails. What we know is that she is against liberal equality, including luck egalitarianism.

Liberal egalitarians are liberal because they think that distributive equality can be reconciled with individual freedom. (Luck egalitarians, such as myself, in addition object to bad brute luck disadvantaging people.) Sypnowich thinks that in their zeal to preserve freedom and choice, liberal egalitarians must endorse a punitive view: once you squander your opportunities, you do not get second chances. She also objects to liberal egalitarians endorsing neutrality—the view that the state must not play favorites between reasonable conceptions of a good life. (In fact, some prominent liberal egalitarians—including G. A. Cohen and Kasper Lippert-Rasmussen—don't endorse neutrality.)

Why be a liberal egalitarian? Suppose we accept that the state ought to make sure that people flourish equally and that this idea has more than limp distributive implications. Flourishing may mean a life genuinely filled with music, as Sypnowich suggests. But it may also mean living in the countryside far away from the crowds. It may mean having children and access to in vitro fertilization (IVF). And so on.

If funding is needed to facilitate IVF there will be less for music. If music is well funded, there will be less for public transport in remote areas. So how should the egalitarian state decide how much to spend on each? One option is a democratic vote: this much for music, this much for IVF, and this much for internet access for remote parts of the country. But why would a vote deliver equality of flourishing rather than privileged funding for the mode of flourishing that majorities enjoy? We avoid such domination if we leave people at least some room to decide for themselves which ends to pursue in life, in conjunction with their communities but not ruled by them.

For this reason, Rawls advocates that each person should enjoy equal expectations of equal income and wealth (unless inequality would benefit the worst off) so that people can make their own choices about their own lives. Dworkin advocates granting each person equal resources: they are equal if each person has a fair opportunity to lead the good life she plans for herself. Contained in these proposals is the idea that if you act in ways that require you to have more than these fair shares—for example, by insisting that only handcrafted gold wallpaper will do—then granting you more would be unfair to others and create, rather than eliminate, inequality. But this attractive idea is miles away from the caricature of liberal egalitarianism according to which those who fare badly in part due to their avoidable choices must bear their fate. Accepting that the avoidability of an outcome may sometimes make a difference to people's entitlements does not entail accepting that it should make much or all the difference.

In fact, as Marc Fleurbaey, Andrew Williams, Serena Olsaretti, Tom Parr, and others (including myself) have argued, there is nothing in the concept of equality of opportunity that requires its proponents to give any weight to choice. The weight that is given can be calibrated such that, for example, choice can never justify disadvantage of a certain type. Everyone can be guaranteed essential medical treatment, decent housing, and a guaranteed income at the bar of liberal egalitarian justice.

So why not guarantee a life filled with music, too? Why leave any room for choice that may leave a person with less than they were shooting for? Because an egalitarian society needs to offer people some (limited) independence from each other. If my access to additional IVF, beyond what everyone might be guaranteed, depends always on how you vote (that is, if majorities decide) or on what you claim for yourself (that is, if you are always entitled to the outcome you pursue), then you are deciding for me far in excess of how far my life should be shaped by the fact that we share our world together.

These ideas about choice don't rest on the simplistic sociological view Sypnowich imagines. First, we should not run together responsibility in the sense of authorship and responsibility in the sense of lacking a complaint against others if an outcome is made to stand. I am often struck by the fact that, although I am the author of the meals I cook, I have a powerful complaint if I have to eat them. Second, attributing choices to people does not mean seeing them as fully separate from their circumstances. It means accepting that agency can be constructed out of the metaphysical mash-up.

Stemplowska

What of the rhetoric of equality of opportunity? A key thing on which Sypnowich and I agree is that Ben Jackson is right: equality of opportunity is a malleable concept. There are conceptions that are disastrous and cruel. But then there are conceptions of equality of outcomes that are disastrous and cruel, too. Egalitarians can argue for limiting people's entitlements so that the choice of a life of music for some does not translate into less medicine for those who would rather have that, without thereby endorsing simplistic sociology. Equal flourishing cannot be secured outside of liberal equality.

THE AMERICAN WAY
Claude Fischer

CHRISTINE SYPNOWICH makes a powerful argument that egalitarians should not settle for better, fairer opportunities but rather campaign for equal outcomes. I agree that equalizing opportunity doesn't equalize well-being, but I get there by a different route—one that leads me to quite different policy suggestions. My vehicle is not philosophy but the social science of inequality and public opinion; I offer a critique not of the morality of the opportunity approach but its practicality. These considerations also raise concerns for Sypnowich's preferred approach.

At one point, Sypnowich asserts that "equal outcomes are in fact what we really care about." The "we" may cover most readers of this magazine, but it excludes most Americans. (I write here only about what I know, which is the United States.) Americans perceive widening economic inequality and complain to pollsters about it, but as sociologist Leslie McCall shows in *The Undeserving Rich* (2013), they overwhelmingly prefer expanding opportunities for upward mobility as the solution. (Americans' major objection to unequal outcomes seems to be that it undermines equal opportunity—not that inequality is in itself immoral, inefficient, or injurious.) Americans were "luck egalitarians" *avant la lettre* and remain so.

But luck egalitarianism offers a weak strategy for attaining equality. For one thing, most parents game every selection system so as to improve their children's life chances through SAT training, multicultural experiences, do-gooder projects, enrichment classes, family connections, funding unpaid internships—whatever it takes. (Sociologist Annette Lareau vividly documents these practices in her 2003 book *Unequal Childhoods*.) Because advantaged parents do these things more and better than disadvantaged parents, expanding opportunities does not do much to weaken intergenerational inequality.

The quest to counterbalance such advantages, to make the race for success ever fairer, leads down a rabbit hole. Recent generations have come to view conditions once thought intrinsic to a person's deserved outcome—race, gender, family background, neighborhood, physical or mental disability, and so on—instead as extrinsic, a matter of luck, a factor that ought to be removed, corrected, or compensated to make the race truly fair. Even economist and former Fed chairman Ben Bernanke described "genetic endowment" as a matter of luck. We increasingly explain variations in ability, tastes, motivation, and even character—e.g., "grit"—as products of biological, environmental, or social luck. (One might well ask: Stripped of all these arbitrary conditions, what is left as the "self" that deserves the fair chance?) As our notion of luck expands, the quest for a luck-free race is never-ending.

More critically, even the fairest race to success yields unequal—increasingly unequal—outcomes. The highest-paid baseball player of 1970, Willie Mays, made eleven times the minimum Major League Baseball wage at the time; the highest-paid player of 2021, Mike Trout, made sixty-five times as much. In modern societies inequality largely resides in the differential rewards for winning or losing, not in the competition itself.

What, then, is a better approach to more equality? Sypnowich insists that we guarantee equal flourishing. How shall we do that? How shall we get consensus to equalize outcomes and find the means to do so? The United States, feared by European elites in the nineteenth century for its distinctive leveling, is now increasingly, distinctively unequal. Economic and institutional structures support that inequality. And so does public opinion.

In 1993 the General Social Survey asked:

> Some people think America should promote equal opportunity for all, that is, allowing everyone to compete for jobs and wealth on a fair and even basis. Other people think America should promote equal outcomes, that is, ensuring that everyone has a decent standard of living and that there are only small differences in wealth and income between the top and bottom in society. Which do you favor: promoting equal opportunity or promoting equal outcomes?

Respondents favored the opportunity option *seven to one*. Since 1984 the quadrennial American National Election Study has asked whether "Our society should do whatever is necessary to make sure that everyone has an equal opportunity to succeed," and over 85 percent of respondents across all years have agreed. (Partisan polarization started to divide the consensus recently.) Only about half have regularly thought that unequal opportunity is a large problem. Surveys show that Americans want to facilitate upward mobility but insist that the assisted be "deserving" of help. At the same time—a Catch-22—Americans typically assume that unsuccessful people are responsible for their failures and are, therefore, undeserving.

American culture poses another problem for Sypnowich's approach. She raises the concern that people may misuse their opportunities and fail to flourish. Her solution, honestly admitted, is to promote citizens' choices in the direction of flourishing—but as decided by whom? The wine, symphony, and hiking crowd, or the beer, wrestling, and gun-range crowd it so often looks down upon? America's democratic spirit still insists that the everyman's judgment is equal to his lordship's. This stance breeds more resistance to the equal flourishing agenda.

In sum, between the power of the powers that be, the grudging luck egalitarianism of Americans, and pushback against a we-know-better elite, how is an equal flourishing agenda to move forward in this country?

One direction is to find ways of leveraging equal opportunity initiatives to effect equal outcomes. Right-wing critiques assert that many purported equal-opportunity moves—affirmative action, eliminating SAT requirements, and the like—are really devices to equalize outcomes. Such techniques have had limited success in doing just that and have also generated backlash against egalitarianism.

Sypnowich nods toward another strategy by concluding, "In short, the egalitarian ideal requires socialism." Good luck with that. Even modest welfare and statist programs are under assault in the West. While socialist urges have found public support—witness the Bernie movement—modest steps taken during the COVID-19 crisis, such as a child allowance, have been terminated with little public blowback. As for the two former bastions of state socialism, China has embraced authoritarian capitalism and Russia has become a brutal kleptocracy.

More pragmatically, American egalitarians could draw on the experiences of nations with more equal human flourishing. In a few books, including *Social Democratic Capitalism* (2019) and *Would Democratic Socialism Be Better?* (2022), sociologist Lane Kenworthy has argued that the Nordic nations provide feasible models that could be replicated here. Denmark and Norway may not be nations of equal flourishing, but with stronger interventions in the market to protect wages and worker well-being and with heavier taxation to sustain income security, universal health care, public child care, and the like, they are a lot closer to that ideal than is the United States.

An agenda focused on public goods—both strengthening them and broadening the category—also has promise. No matter how ideologically conservative, Americans have accepted some social provisioning as public necessities: universal education, national parks, and old-age security, for example. More is possible, from health care to housing and perhaps even guaranteed employment. Successful philosophical justifications for such programs are more likely to be found in the universalist language of human rights than in Marxist-flavored egalitarianism.

While Americans endorse egalitarianism in rights, dignity, and opportunity, they still want competitions that result in inequality. That fact, along with other realities, calls for modesty in goals and programs. An American welfare state that looked more like Northern Europe—where Mike Trout would be more like Willie Mays—would not be a utopia, but it would be better for many people.

HOW TO PROMOTE FLOURISHING
Lane Kenworthy

I AM SYMPATHETIC to Christine Sypnowich's view that flourishing is at the core of what we want in a good society. She's far from alone. To cite just one example, a recent European Commission report on the future of the welfare state contends that

> welfare provision should not merely be assessed in terms of its impact on people's material conditions, but even more so in terms of fostering people's capability to fulfil personal aspirations. Slowly at first, social citizenship values have gradually shifted. Fairness is less likely to be seen as being about 'here-and-now' compensation, and more about how to pro-actively ensure 'human flourishing' and well-being.

What institutions and policies are most conducive to flourishing? We have a good bit of evidence on this, and that evidence suggests the Nordic model—I call it "social democratic capitalism"—does quite well. It features political democracy, a mixed but mostly capitalist economy, good basic education, expansive and generous public insurance programs, employment-friendly public services, and moderate regulation of product and labor markets.

Something approximating this model has been in place in Denmark, Norway, and Sweden for four or five decades, and in Finland for several. Other rich democratic nations have embraced it to a lesser degree. Across those countries, greater commitment to this model is associated with better economic security, higher living standards for the least well-off, and more equality of opportunity for economic success. And this is achieved without sacrificing other elements of a good society, from freedom and economic growth to family, community, and much more.

How does this set of policies and institutions promote flourishing? Three ways are particularly noteworthy.

First, it ensures everyone has access to a variety of key goods and services at little or no cost: safety, water, food (school breakfast and lunch), health care, child care, preschool, elementary school, secondary school, college (zero tuition), job training, job placement assistance, housing assistance, disability services, transportation, information (internet, libraries), legal rights and representation, financial safeguards such as bank deposit insurance and bankruptcy protection, public spaces such as parks and museums, disaster prevention and relief, eldercare, and more.

Second, it cushions against many of life's risks. Paid parental leave, child care, preschool, and a child allowance help with the cost and time burden of childrearing. Training, apprenticeships, job placement assistance, an earnings subsidy (like the Earned Income Tax Credit), a guaranteed minimum income, retraining, and lifelong learning boost the labor market opportunities of people who struggle with school and increase incomes for those with low earnings. Unemployment insurance, sickness insurance, and disability payments help to ensure that if you aren't able to work, or can't work as much as you'd like, your income won't drop too much. Retirement pensions and eldercare ensure that when your work years are finished you won't live in poverty or lack needed assistance.

Third, it facilitates and encourages paid work. I've already mentioned many of the key supports. There are also supports for flexible working hours along with mandates for thirty or so paid vacation days and holidays each year. Employment doesn't contribute to flourishing for everyone, but it does help many people. And we need a lot of adults in paid work to fund abundant public goods and services and insurance programs without exorbitant tax rates.

This doesn't guarantee that every person will find their soulmate and their calling and live blissfully for 115 years. But it does ensure that everyone has much of what's needed for a life that is fulfilling. Life tends to be stunted when people have to spend much of their day worrying about their personal safety, driving for hours to and from a job, or fearing they'll be unable to pay the rent, get needed medical treatment, or afford child care. These types of concerns dominate mental bandwidth, cause stress and anxiety, impede long-term thinking and planning, and make change risky. Thankfully, we have the knowledge and the resources to remove these and other impediments for nearly everyone.

The total cost of public programs, goods, services, and government operations amounts to about half of an affluent country's gross domestic product. For most households in these countries, somewhere between one-third and half of income goes to the government in taxes.

Skeptics on the left sometimes suggest that social democratic capitalism peaked in the 1960s and 1970s, retreating since then in the face of a business offensive and economic globalization. But that's mistaken. In fact, it's precisely during the post-1970s period that the Nordic countries solidified a policy approach coupling a big welfare state with employment promotion. And key outcomes haven't worsened. Many have improved.

Not only has social democratic capitalism worked very well up to now. It also is well positioned to face some key challenges that lie ahead, including population aging, economic globalization, and the weakening of family and civic organizations. Let me highlight two others.

First, advances in automation and the rise of the gig and platform economies have increased work flexibility but also precariousness. This may cause more people to fear losing their jobs, move in and out of jobs, work irregularly, or work multiple jobs. In this environment, individuals and households will be more economically secure if benefits and insurance are generous and provided by government. Think of a stereotypical member of the modern precariat, working irregular shifts at a coffee shop and driving for an on-demand ride service. In the contemporary United States, such a life can be semi-hellish—low-income, unpredictable, at the mercy of finicky managers and customers. Now imagine it where every person has the kinds of public services and goods and insurance I've described here.

In this latter context, while irregular or low-paid employment may still be suboptimal, it will be noticeably less stressful and problematic.

Second, what about robots and artificial intelligence replacing jobs currently performed by humans? As this plays out, more and more of us will work in in-person service positions—caring, repairing, healing, cooking, cleaning, teaching, training, mentoring, coaching, counseling, advising, planning, organizing. (In other words, the kinds of services upper-middle-class Americans currently purchase for themselves, their children, and their elderly parents.) People in these types of jobs will have a greater ability to flourish, to have a good life, if they are supported by an array of goods, services, benefits, and insurance programs that are guaranteed by government.

Social democratic capitalism doesn't achieve, or even aim for, the equality of flourishing Sypnowich favors. It's something closer to equality of opportunity for flourishing, though with a recognition that ensuring such opportunity (or, if you prefer, capability) continues throughout the life course. Once we get closer to genuinely equal opportunity for flourishing, we'll be in a better position to decide whether it's feasible, and if so desirable, to aim for equality of actual flourishing.

In short: if affluent countries, and perhaps also middle-income ones, want to promote flourishing, they should start by copying the Nordic model.

OUTCOMES SHAPE OPPORTUNITIES

Gina Schouten

CHRISTINE SYPNOWICH is right that an egalitarian society should be concerned with egalitarian outcomes. But she's wrong to reject equal opportunity as the fundamental goal which motivates that concern. As I see it, egalitarians should care about people living equally flourishing lives *because* egalitarians should care about people having equal opportunities to flourish.

This claim might sound odd because opportunity equality is conventionally contrasted with outcome equality. But in fact, the two converge in substance. Our moral concern should be for equal opportunity, and genuinely equal opportunity requires a great deal of outcome equality.

Let me begin my case with three observations about equal opportunity.

First, there are two distinct questions that left liberals might answer by advancing opportunity egalitarianism. The first concerns fundamental entitlements of distributive fairness: What is each person due as a matter of basic justice? The second concerns the arrangement of social institutions: What principles ought to guide the design of our social arrangement? These are distinct questions: while our fundamental entitlements of justice surely matter to the design of our social arrangement, they are arguably not *all* that matters. Perhaps the social arrangement should secure fundamental entitlements *only* as far as is consistent with democratic legitimacy, for instance.

In response to the first question, my own answer is: we are all entitled to enjoy equal opportunities to live flourishing lives. In response to the second question, my answer is: *one* principle that ought to guide our social arrangement directs social institutions to work together to equalize developmental opportunities (e.g., through progressive education) and to undermine the influence of social class background on our prospects for leading flourishing lives (e.g., through economic justice measures like inheritance taxation). In other words, social institutions ought to work together to equalize developmental and competitive opportunity. By virtue of these two answers, I'm a proponent of equal opportunity twice over.

A second observation is that equal opportunity is a distributive rule that favors equal opportunities *for* something; it leaves open the question of what that something is. Sypnowich emphasizes that her outcome egalitarianism regulates the distribution of flourishing. But opportunity egalitarians are entitled to conjoin their distributive rule with a flourishing metric of justice, just as outcome egalitarians are. Hence my formulation above: I think we are all fundamentally entitled by justice to equal *opportunities* to live *flourishing* lives.

Now for my third observation. Egalitarians of all stripes think that some outcome inequalities are objectionable inequalities. Sypnowich thinks that outcome egalitarianism impugns more inequality than opportunity egalitarianism, and that this fact counts in its favor. But quantifying this divergence depends upon descriptive facts about the social world we inhabit. To the extent that outcome inequality results from or causes unequal opportunity, opportunity egalitarianism coincides with outcome egalitarianism in condemning inequality.

Together, these observations weaken Sypnowich's case against equal opportunity.

Consider equal opportunity as an answer to the first question, about the fundamental entitlements of justice. Opportunities are unequal, on my view, when we flourish less than others due to causes for which we're non-responsible. For which flourishing deficits are we non-responsible? Here, as Sypnowich points out, we enter the difficult terrain of free will, determinism, and social influences on seemingly voluntary choice. My own conviction is that vanishingly few inequalities pass the test for responsibility. Sypnowich seems to agree: "If the individual is embedded in a complex weave of social factors, it is poor sociology to conceive of the ideal society as one where individuals enjoy absolute authority over judgments of value." Critics of opportunity egalitarianism spill much ink pointing out the flaws in this bit of "poor sociology." But opportunity egalitarianism is not a sociological claim, nor does it entail a sociological claim. We must distinguish the normative issue—whether and why inequality is unjust—from the descriptive one: how much responsibility we in fact have.

These are independent questions, however much they are run together in political rhetoric; a moral commitment to equal opportunity says nothing, in itself, about what we are responsible for. I agree with Sypnowich's sociology, and it tells me something about which inequalities equal opportunity impugns: if the complex weave of social factors within which we live makes fully responsible choice exceedingly rare, then equal opportunity dictates that unequal outcomes are *exceedingly rarely just.*

Now consider the second question, about how we should arrange social institutions. I've endorsed an equal opportunity principle that favors equalizing developmental opportunity. But equal developmental opportunity is (at best) very difficult to achieve in unequal societies precisely because advantaged parents find ways to give their own children a developmental leg up. This intergenerational transfer of advantage (and disadvantage) means that unequal outcomes obstruct equal developmental opportunity. And *that* means equal opportunity impugns the unequal outcomes that disrupt it. As a principle guiding the arrangement of social institutions, equal opportunity favors equal outcomes as a means of preserving equal developmental opportunities.

Equal opportunity is radically egalitarian. Egalitarians *should* be concerned about outcomes. But this is because equal opportunity captures the basic entitlements of justice, because vanishingly few outcome inequalities are fully attributable to individual responsibility, and because unequal outcomes themselves contribute to unequal opportunities. What's unjust is still unequal *opportunity*. Only when the facts on the ground reveal that virtually all outcome inequality implicates opportunity inequality do we see that virtually all significant outcome inequality constitutes a failure of justice: a failure to secure equal opportunity.

If outcome and opportunity egalitarianism converge in regarding a great deal of inequality as unjust, why not dispense with opportunity talk? I see two reasons not to.

First, in some contexts, accuracy matters, and the convergence between the two forms of egalitarianism is not *total*. Responsibility plausibly comes in degrees, and degree of responsibility might matter when resources are scarce. People can flourish in different ways of life, and most of us need some trial and error to find a good fit. We're plausibly entitled by justice to second and third chances to live flourishing lives when one life path fails to pan out. But do basic entitlements of justice favor a subsidy of someone's fourth chance over someone else's first? What if the fourth chancer was born into privilege relative to the first chancer? If we're even marginally responsible in even *some* cases of failed experiments in living, that can affect how strongly we're entitled to social subsidy when our subsidy would come at a cost to someone else's and when we've enjoyed greater subsidy already. Only equal *opportunity* can explain this plausible conviction *and* the egalitarian convictions on which I agree with Sypnowich.

Second, if we care about democratic community, we cannot pursue equality by just *any* means at our disposal. We must build a democratic constituency in favor of equality, for which equal opportunity is a powerful tool. Many citizens reject Sypnowich's and my socialist commitments. They might nonetheless endorse equal opportunity as a principle to guide our social arrangement. If so, then building a democratic constituency for socialist reform doesn't require settling first principles. It only requires that we make visible the sociological facts in virtue of which a shared first principle favors more equal outcomes. Socialist egalitarians should retain equal opportunity as the moral goal that motivates their concern for equal outcomes. Equal opportunity is radically egalitarian, and it can serve as a shared premise in public political deliberation.

EQUALITY MATTERS
Christine Sypnowich

IT IS A TESTAMENT to the power of the ideal of equality, and to the extent to which liberal democratic societies are failing to achieve it, that this forum has attracted such a range of outstanding responses.

The contributors and I all agree that we live in societies marked by inequality, that this is wrong, and that something should be done about it. But we have different ideas about how to understand those convictions. I argue that the idea of equality of opportunity, a foundational principle of much egalitarianism, is inadequate. It leads to distributive policies guided by the principle that only individual choice should affect people's share of goods and that therefore widely diverging lots in life can be just. In other words, equal opportunity is consistent with significant inequality in income, health, education, and many other sources of well-being. Instead of equality of opportunity, I argue, we should focus on how well people are doing—that is, whether they are flourishing.

One group of critics insists that equality of opportunity is more radical, at least potentially, than I give it credit for. John Roemer, one of its leading progressive exponents, says that properly understood, equality of opportunity is "neither left- nor right-wing," as its redistributive potential depends on the goals that a society decides to set. Choice is of negligible importance if social conditions largely consist in circumstances beyond people's control, particularly in the case of children, whose inequalities should be understood solely as a matter of circumstance. Martin O'Neill makes a powerful pitch for Rawls's idea of "fair equality of opportunity," which, he contends, promises far-reaching egalitarian polices, such as aggressive taxation of inheritance and capital transfer and, indeed, the "abolition of social class." Gina Schouten also persuasively contends that equality of opportunity can set a high bar for egalitarianism—converging with that envisaged by a focus on outcomes—and, moreover, can have flourishing as its object.

A second group of critics, such as Claude Fischer and to a lesser degree Leah Gordon, reflecting on the inhospitable American scene past and present, provide sobering counsel that a focus on outcomes could be political suicide. Given the popular appeal of ideas like merit, private property, and social mobility, it is only prudent for egalitarians to adopt modest goals and focus on equality of opportunity. Schouten similarly stresses the need to build "a democratic constituency," which may mean lowering our sights. A common theme is that liberal democratic societies have not even attained the amelioration of disadvantage promised by the opportunity principle, so complaining that opportunity approaches are too modest looks utopian.

The two lines of criticism are in tension. If equality of opportunity is really so radical, why does it appeal to political realists? In my view, if we heed the realists' advice, we risk capitulating to a grudging outlook that is unwilling to remedy disadvantage that, though ostensibly the result of free choices, is mired in unchosen and unjust social conditions. It is important not to obscure the distinction between what is feasible and what justice requires. That a robust egalitarian policy does not find favor in public discourse or at the polls does not necessarily tell against its merit. Ravi Kanbur warns that if a seat at the policymaking table involves embracing more widely palatable but inadequate views, that could serve to undermine the spirit of egalitarianism altogether.

My view that human flourishing should be the focus of our egalitarianism is also controversial. Yet it is endorsed by two quite contrasting perspectives. William Paris makes an eloquent appeal for cultivating the "art of equality" and the utopianism of the egalitarian ideal. At the same time, Kanbur agrees with me that outcomes matter, providing a strong case for the importance of functionings rather than opportunities to function. It is pleasing to see that the flourishing approach garners the approval of both a self-avowed utopian as well as an exponent of the dismal science (not so dismal in Kanbur's hands!).

Anne Phillips and Nicholas Vrousalis, however, balk at what they see as the paternalism inherent in talk of flourishing, counseling that egalitarians should instead tackle the structural inequalities of capitalism and respect the freedom of people—particularly the oppressed—to make their own choices. That socialists harbor liberal anxieties about affirming visions of the good is surprising. I agree that structural inequalities give people little in the way of real choice about how their lives should go, but surely we draw that conclusion in light of the poor outcomes that people are forced to live with. It is because putatively "free" choices produce such appalling outcomes that the structural inequalities of capitalism should stand condemned. Marx's understanding of socialism was not so squeamish; it involved, besides the elimination of material deprivation, the cultivation of creative activity, solidarity, and liberation from alienation.

Zofia Stemplowska raises the important worry that questions about plans of life are too controversial to be decided by a community on behalf of its members. Who is to say that music is more central to human flourishing than parenting—IVF-assisted, if necessary? Yet in fact, liberal democratic capitalist societies, for all their inequalities, do seek to foster human well-being in a range of public policies. The arts are subsidized. Public libraries lend books for free. IVF treatment is in fact funded, at least in part, by socialized medicine in Canada, the UK, and other European countries. For those students whose families cannot afford or are disinclined to lay on music lessons, the experience of choir, musical theater, or the school band can be life changing. Their provision in publicly funded schools is recognition not just, as Gordon and Roemer stress, that we should tackle disadvantage among children, but also that human flourishing attends certain pursuits. In contrast to the doctrines of many liberal theorists, liberal democratic societies are often prepared to take a stand on what contributes to human flourishing and is properly within the purview of public provision, prohibition, and subsidy.

Moreover, shouldn't the "chancers," as Schouten puts it, who mess up repeatedly, nonetheless have their needs met? The suggestion that anti-vaxxers who failed to take appropriate precautions be denied medical treatment if they caught COVID-19 was an understandable reaction, especially given the scarcity of medical resources, but it did not pass egalitarian muster. Of course, no one in the present company is against guaranteed essential medical treatment, as Stemplowska points out. Yet this raises the question of what work ideas of choice, responsibility, and opportunity are doing in a properly generous understanding of the egalitarian ideal.

Unconditional, free medical care for all is a significant achievement of the Nordic model extolled by Lane Kenworthy (and noted by utopia-wary Fischer). This model involves universally available programs and services, from health care to parks—a strategy that meets the needs of all members of society but also fosters solidarity, which in turn strengthens citizens' commitment to these policies. As Kenworthy points out, public goods approaches are remarkably successful. Of course, they depend on a preparedness to determine the good that should be provided publicly—in other words, deciding what in fact contributes to human flourishing.

To conclude, it seems a sad comment that the egalitarian project is so often understood as a matter of determining the terms of competition for hierarchically distributed positions and rewards. Such a view seems a betrayal of the idea of an egalitarian community committed to the well-being of each member. I hope to have rekindled radical hope for the socialist values demanded by a robust understanding of equality. Nonetheless, in this dispiriting time of profound inequality, poverty, homelessness, and the deterioration of many people's standard of living, it is gratifying to see the compelling arguments of this forum which, however diverse, share a passionate commitment to the egalitarian ideal.

ESSAYS

THE NEOLIBERAL CAPTURE OF EDUCATION POLICY

Christopher Newfield

A LONG TIME AGO the United States had a civil rights enforcement system that increased racial equality.

Generations of Black critique and social movements finally led, in the late 1950s, to federally mandated voluntary desegregation agreements, but these accomplished very little. Many momentous events later, policy frameworks emerged in the mid-1960s that did have a meaningful impact. In 1963 John F. Kennedy proposed the Civil Rights Act that Lyndon Johnson, propelled by a relentless civil rights movement, finally pushed through a Congress that stalled it for weeks in 1964. A month after it was passed came the Economic Opportunity Act, the cornerstone of the federal War on Poverty. The following year saw the Elementary and Secondary Education Act (the first general funding program for education in federal history) and the first Higher Education Act. By the end of this period the United States had laws prohibiting racial segregation and discrimination in several key arenas of national life, including housing, hospitality, education, employment, and elections.

Yet laws alone still weren't enough. In his new book, *The Walls around Opportunity*, Gary Orfield—a leading scholar of civil rights in education—shows that what did work was straightforward legal and budgetary coercion. School districts would no longer be able to file desegregation plans and go home with an A for effort. Civil rights lawyers no longer had to sue each segregated school district one at a time; legislation authorized class-action lawsuits and the withholding of federal funds from any entity that failed to produce measurable progress toward desegregation. Perhaps in part because the United States was a nation created, expanded, and maintained through the use of force, it was force, legal and fiscal, that finally got results—at least for a brief historical moment.

As education economists Sandy Baum and Michael McPherson demonstrate in *Can College Level the Playing Field?*, that moment has passed. The authors usefully document yawning gaps in opportunity among economic and racial groups at every stage of life in the United States today, and they make two startling points about any possible remedies. First, improvements will require cooperation of all "our major social and economic institutions"—including all levels of education, which would be without precedent in U.S. history. Second, economic policy has pushed unequal opportunity to such extremes that reversing it "will be the work of generations."

And yet, instead of systematically developing solutions as big as the problems they identify, the authors build toward the resigned conclusion that higher education policy can do little in light of the daunting "extent of the structural inequalities facing people throughout their lives." They are right that colleges cannot do everything.

But in the absence of a substantial argument about what needs to be done, this cautionary moral is more likely to function as an alibi for the status quo than to inspire action capable of meeting the structural challenge. Given their pallid endings, both books call on us to explore the roots of the policy paralysis that accompanies their clear vision of our inequality crisis.

ORFIELD PRESENTS a stark historical portrait of educational injustice. As he documents in detail, when U.S. states were left to their own discretion, they created a coast-to-coast tableau of discrimination in schooling. In the mid-1940s nearly half of Latino children in Texas had no education of any kind; in 1950 the average educational attainment of Southwest Latinos was less than the sixth grade. In 1964, Orfield reports, "there were still five southern states where at least 97 percent of the Black students were attending Black colleges." This was true for three-quarters of Black students in the South overall. Schooling in the North and West was also largely segregated, if more informally, and financially unequal. Only limited progress had been made on higher education integration since 1910. (Up to that year, W. E. B. Du Bois noted, white colleges had graduated 693 Black students in all of U.S. history.) The segregated South of separate drinking fountains was only the most visible part of a spectrum of apartheid variations across the country that affected every aspect of daily life, also generating racially disparate wages and wealth accumulation during the economic boom following World War II.

Newfield

The mid-1960s were the first meaningful turning point toward racial integration at least since the end of Reconstruction in 1877. Civil rights enforcement—in which the federal government was not only enabled but required to sue or defund discrimination—formally delegitimated American-as-apple-pie racial segregation in education. It sought an end to Black exclusion from white schools, starting with supporting the rights of Black students to transfer to white schools (already at issue in *Brown v. Board of Education* in 1954). By 1968, in *Green v. County Sch. Bd. of New Kent County*, the Supreme Court affirmed the goal of ending "dual school systems, part 'white' and part 'Negro'" and replacing them with a "unitary, nonracial" system in which each school would be too integrated to be identified with a clearly dominant race.

The idea wasn't to integrate U.S. society at large, however, but only to eradicate race-based schools. Different schools might still produce unequal outcomes—different average test scores and graduation rates—just not because there were white or Black schools. Coupled with infusions of federal funding that was specifically set aside for poor and vulnerable populations, schools were expected to have sufficiently similar financial means as well as demographics to allow any school system to be unitary in fact.

Mandatory racial integration became both the means and an ethical and sociocultural end in itself. It is notable that progress was measured by a growing equality of results. Between 1975–76 and 1980–81, Orfield observes, "the percentage of Southern Black graduates receiving their bachelor's degrees from predominantly white institutions rose by a third" (and rose, though more slowly, outside the South). "For a brief period in the late 1970s, a Black high school graduate was about as likely as a white one to start college." The share of Black people between the ages of 25 and 29 with a B.A. degree doubled during the 1960s, from 5.4 percent to 10 percent (it had also doubled in the 1950s from 2.8 percent). High school degrees for the same age cohort went from just under 40 percent to just under 60 percent in the 1960s, and grew to 77 percent through the 1970s. In other words, the movement toward racial equality—and our ongoing failure to achieve it—has been measured in the language not of opportunities but of outcomes: of closing racial gaps in graduation rates, wages, family wealth, and the like.

These gains prompted backlash. The right had been geared up against integration since *Brown v. Board of Education* in 1954 and was ready to fight these new federal mandates. Conservatives quickly racked up major political victories—Ronald Reagan's election as California governor in 1966, Richard Nixon's win of the White House in 1968 and repeat in 1972, and then Reagan's ascent to the presidency in 1981. Economist Thomas Piketty has noted that wages grew as fast or faster than investment income for at most five decades in capitalism's history, all in the middle of the twentieth century. Orfield sees a far more limited window of serious civil rights enforcement, lasting from 1965 to 1970. Civil rights funding carried on through the 1970s, aimed at increasingly voluntary programs, but that too mostly ended with Reagan's presidency in 1981.

Nixon was able to appoint four conservative justices to the Supreme Court, which began to qualify civil rights rather than enforce them. In 1973 a 5–4 majority decided there was no constitutional right to equal school funding, undermining the material basis of equal outcomes. In 1974 it "ruled that a city's suburbs could not be included in desegregation plans even when that was the only way to remedy a history of segregation." This effectively endorsed white flight and residential segregation as end-runs around racially unitary school districts. In 1978 the Court decided that colleges could use affirmative action to enhance diversity for educational purposes but not to remedy a history of racial discrimination. This transformed the integration of university student bodies and faculty from a mandatory affair to a voluntary one, to be pursued at the discretion of the largely white officials who ran highly selective institutions. In 1991 and 1992 the Court ruled that federal desegregation orders can be ended if a district has ended past discriminatory practices and has been complying with the order in good faith. This pushed the closing of racial gaps back toward the pre-1960s terrain of a voluntary effort. In 2007 the Court ruled such "voluntary efforts of local communities illegal if students were selected on the basis of race, even in pursuit of maintaining integration opportunities in largely segregated communities." Similar decisions were taking place in parallel in employment law and in other areas.

By the early 1990s conservatives had thus made racial integration optional once more. They redefined equal treatment as the duty *not* to use race as a policy category. Their alleged constitutional principle of colorblindness helped them to discredit the systematic measurement of outcome gaps across racial groups by bringing the category of race itself into disrepute. In California, Governor Pete Wilson convinced voters to outlaw affirmative action by burying data about the underrepresentation of Black and Latino students at the University of California in Berkeley and LA beneath a mountain of outrage that race was considered in admissions at all. The operational definition of a civil right was returned to state and other local officials; integration and parity in funding, graduation rates, and college qualification again depended on the good will of the managers of the various systems.

These preferences would best be sorted out through markets, the argument went, with government playing a minimal background role. Quality of outcomes would be best judged by the flow of private investments, and if this led to charter schools and further segregation, then so be it; this was the "freedom to choose" so central to American capitalism and democracy. Reagan famously said that "government is not the solution to our problem; government is the problem." Markets were Reagan's solution: they would allow individuals to make their *own* decisions about housing, schooling, transportation, and the like. If capitalism was racialized, well, it wasn't racism's fault; it was just money and freedom. And government was not to interfere with either.

The all too familiar result has been a dramatic dismantling of Great Society gains—what Orfield has long called *resegregation*. "School segregation for both Blacks and Latinos has continuously increased since 1991," he reports. In California in 1970 "the typical Latino had been in a majority-white school." Now, Latino students in California on average "attend schools with only about a sixth whites and a great majority of fellow students living in poverty." In the United States in 2016–17, "Black and Latino students were, on average, attending schools that were three-fourths nonwhite and with substantial majorities of children living in poverty, while white and Asian students were in middle-class schools." In concurrence, Baum and McPherson use federal data to show that between 1995 and 2017, the share of Black students in schools at least three-quarters white has been cut by more than half, from an already small 11 percent down to 4 percent. The same has happened to Latino students. Black high school graduation rates among 25 to 29-year-olds moved from 77 percent to just 82 percent during the 1980s and didn't reach 90 percent until 2013—the level achieved by whites in 1990. Over sixty years after *Brown*, a large share of students of color (excepting Asians) start from "double segregation," isolated in schools with fewer resources in communities suffering the same conditions. The "unitary" school district is mere legend for the vast majority of U.S. students.

Something similar happened at colleges and universities. Since 1995 about three-quarters of Latino, Black, and indigenous students have attended underfunded colleges with low graduation rates compared to only about half of white students. Meanwhile, about half of white and most Asian American students have gone to wealthier schools with higher graduation rates. In 2019 bachelor degree attainment for 25 to 29 year olds was 72 percent and 45 percent for Asians and whites, and 26 percent and 23 percent for Black and Latino students.

The crucial metric is expenditures per student, and the gaps are very large. "The 82 most selective colleges spend almost five times as much and the most selective 468 colleges spend twice as much on instruction per student as the open-access schools," a Georgetown University study has shown. And these are averages; gaps between the most selective universities like Stanford and Princeton and the rest are far larger.

In their third chapter, Baum and McPherson note a similar pattern. A major 2013 report that demonstrated this pattern was aptly titled "Separate and Unequal" and subtitled, "How Higher Education Reinforces the Intergenerational Reproduction of White Racial Privilege." It should have provoked national action to equalize cross-racial outcomes by equalizing funding, but it did not. Students of color did expand their share of college degrees after 1995, but this reflected demographic change more than additional investment in closing gaps in graduation rates. To the contrary, this was precisely the period in which public funding for higher education stagnated or fell, leaving most underrepresented students to their own devices—meaning more borrowing, more work during term, more overcrowded or precarious housing, and more visits to foodbanks.

WHAT HAPPENED to civil rights momentum? A large and often brilliant literature has taken up this topic. One recurring theme is that the blunting of educational justice has been a bipartisan affair. The enabling framework was a reassertion of market control over social policy: "freedom to choose" for the Republicans, "learn to earn" and "education for growth" for the Democrats. Within that framework, three mechanisms are particularly notable.

The first was the failure of the primal desegregation decisions, *Brown v. Board of Education* I and II (1954 and 1955, respectively), to link desegregation to equality of resource outcomes. Legal scholar Cheryl I. Harris has argued that though the Court declared that separate is inherently unequal, "it remained unwilling to embrace any form of substantive equality, unwilling to acknowledge any right to equality of resources." The *Brown* theory was that "inequality would be eradicated by desegregation." If all students arrived to schools on a non-racial basis, then any remaining inequalities would not be attributable to racism—and the Court's interest ended there. Never mind that predominantly white school districts might receive radically more funding than predominantly Black school districts, thanks in part to extreme variations in property values (and the wedding of school funding to local taxes). On this view, that isn't racism; it's just federalism and free association. In the words of scholar Alan Freeman, under *Brown* "there is no recognized right, no ethical claim for equality of resources or a substantively effective education as such." This very much included the material inequalities between Black and white Americans that derived both from segregation and dispossession in the past and enduring deprivation in the present.

Harris did not see *Brown*'s original sin of omission as a mere oversight. Enduring inequality of material resources is the essence of white entitlement—what she calls "whiteness as property." We now often use the term "racial capitalism" to name the inequality generated by the workings of a U.S. economy built around structural racial disparities in wealth, wages, housing, education, and other social resources. Neither the Warren Court nor civil rights liberalism confronted it.

The second move was to fuse education with economic performance while blaming teachers and liberal values for any inadequacy. The economic alarm was sounded by a federal report called "A Nation at Risk" (1983). Claiming that the country's "mediocre educational performance" looks like what a foreign power might impose in an "act of war," the report blew the trumpets of impending economic disaster. The cause? U.S. schools were not driving their students to compete with those from Germany, Japan, and South Korea in the knowledge economy. Among many others, its rather unhinged language was taken up by William Bennett, Reagan's chair of the National Endowment for the Humanities and Secretary of Education, to create a nationwide pressure campaign to monitor schools. Reagan read the report as saying what he wanted to hear, which was that liberalism had led to "two decades in which money had been the only measure of progress in education, and in which, while Federal spending on education went steadily up, test scores fell steadily down and too many schools accepted the fashions of the day—the fashions of liberal culture—that held traditional standards in scorn."

Reagan asserted these things at an event in 1988 for a Department of Education report entitled "American Education: Making it Work." His administration simply buried the problems of segregation and racial inequality of educational outcomes, replacing them with the alleged problems of indulgent, liberal teachers, race consciousness, and too much government money, which would be fixed by imposing external standards, bringing in school vouchers, encouraging private schools and public subsidies for them, cutting public funds, and disciplining teachers who couldn't get test results. As we all know now, the Reagan-era rollback failed at its official goal, which was to improve educational outcomes. In 2017 the United States ranked twelfth in degree attainment in OECD statistics, with one of the smallest rates of improvement in the forty-eight countries tracked. But Reaganism succeeded at its unofficial goal, which was to redefine civil rights as a burden to economic prosperity, social order, and the white majority.

What made Reaganism especially damaging, however, was that Bill Clinton and Barack Obama accepted most of it. In the 1990s Clinton assembled liberal experts who called for the regeneration of America through globalization and technology, not equality and justice. In 2002 George W. Bush signed the No Child Left Behind Act, implementing a punishing regime of high-stakes testing in K–12 education that cast schools and teachers—rather than wide-spread inequality—as the problem, and through the Department of Education's Race to the Top program, launched in 2009 just six months after taking office, Obama kept Bush's focus on identifying underperforming schools as well as teachers classed as failures on the basis of test scores. Throughout the Obama years, Orfield notes, teachers still tried to avoid stigmatized schools and worked under controlled curricula where learning was defined down as the students' successful reproduction of test materials. Late in his second term Obama signed the Every Student Succeeds Act, which eliminated some aspects of Bush's high-stakes testing—the implementation at the federal level—but also dramatically curtailed the role of the federal government in educational oversight across the board, largely returning the issue to the states.

Neither Clinton nor Obama pushed unionized wages in order to diminish the "college premium" or supported racially unitary school districts through equalized funding. Neither administration pounded away on the themes of structural racism, underdevelopment, or the need for equitable funding of public schools. And both administrations accepted the Republican definition of affirmative action as a "thumb on the scale" of objective merit rather than criticizing the fundamental structure of meritocracy as an engine of social and economic inequality. In short, the Democratic Party capitulated to the Reaganite vision: rather than viewing education as a public good—for equal outcomes regardless of private means—it has gone on making education dependent on private resources and market choices, all while pretending that education—not "labor unions or a progressive tax code," say—is "the key to addressing economic inequality," as Jennifer Berkshire and Jack Schneider recently put it. In this post-Reagan Democratic consensus, learning is still above all about earning, and justice simply requires continuous performance audits of teachers and students, all for the sake of market-led growth. The inequality boom has been the predictable result.

Higher education has suffered a similar fate. Over the last several decades, public universities have accepted state cuts in large part because it was harder to fight the statehouse than to raise tuition on students. In 1995 states on average allocated $8,922 per "full-time equivalent student." In 2020 that figure was $8,636, below the 1995 level adjusted for inflation. Public college students spent much of the 2010s getting allocations that were 10–20 percent below those of 1995. The federal government accepted a dramatic drop in the relative value of its main grant, the Pell grant, and a shift of financial aid from grants to loans. It let a good chunk of the federal loan system be siphoned off by for-profit colleges, leading disproportionate shares of students of color toward the worst graduation rates, highest debt loads, and highest default rates in known higher education history. Cuts particularly hurt the lower-cost colleges students of color and poor students disproportionately attend, reducing the kind of educational contact, small classes, and permanent faculty that increase learning. State colleges jacked up tuition, often at a faster pace than the privates, which still didn't cover losses to instructional budgets, encouraging the adjunctification of the professoriat.

Administrators looked to edtech as a magic bullet, treating online education as if it made reinvestment in public colleges unnecessary—even when results were inferior to face-to-face instruction, particularly for Black and Latino students. This highly unequal system was legitimated by the rankings industry, which made enormously uneven status and outcomes seem a natural feature of a competitive system rather than the problem that the civil rights movement had tried to fix. Most people disliked pretty much all of these trends. Noting the drops in public confidence in the value of a college degree, education economists began to re-rank colleges via their contribution to social mobility (another name for upward mobility), a zero-sum game that further eclipsed the vision of egalitarian improvement across the board. In short, post-1990 higher ed policy has steadily eroded the material conditions of civil rights, even as diversity, equity, and inclusion remain solemn goals.

These first two moves away from racial equality—condoning wealth inequality as an inevitable consequence of freedom and redefining education in terms of economic results—have had significant but well-documented effects. Perhaps even more insidious is the third move: a retreat to equal opportunity as somehow separable from equal outcomes. And it is on this third move that both books are most disappointing. Indeed, they exemplify it.

EQUALITY OF OPPORTUNITY has been a mainstream policy goal for years now, and it is the ethical horizon of these two arguments—the "level playing field" of Baum and McPherson's title. But a different mainstream operated in the mid-1960s, one that saw equal opportunity as the means to the end of equal outcomes. That goal appeared in a famous commencement address Lyndon Johnson delivered at Howard University in 1965:

> Freedom is the right to share, share fully and equally, in American society—to vote, to hold a job, to enter a public place, to go to school. It is the right to be treated in every part of our national life as a person equal in dignity and promise to all others.
>
> But freedom is not enough. . . . You do not take a person who, for years, has been hobbled by chains and liberate him, bring him up to the starting line of a race and then say, "You are free to compete with all the others," and still justly believe that you have been completely fair.
>
> Thus it is not enough just to open the gates of opportunity. All our citizens must have the ability to walk through those gates. And this is the next and the more profound stage of the battle for civil rights.
>
> We seek not just freedom but opportunity. We seek not just legal equity but human ability, not just equality as a right and a theory, but equality as a fact, and equality as a result.

Johnson defined equal opportunity as the gateway to equal results. This could not mean that every individual would end up with equal resources, but it did mean that equal outcomes should hold across racial *groups*. On average, Black students would graduate from high school at roughly the same rates as whites, go on to university at the same rates, get bachelor's degrees at the same rates, and so on. (The same would be true of indigenous and Latino students—indeed students from any racial group.) With visible and structural inequalities truly undone, Blacks as a group would come to earn, on average, the same as whites in employment after college, and their family wealth would soon become comparable (rather than get stuck at 15 percent of white wealth, where it has lingered for years). A similar line of thought lay behind the Equal Rights Amendment to the Constitution: women should earn the same as men. On this conception, justice entails not the right to *compete* to be equal—as had been done for centuries—but being equal *in fact*.

Johnson said the quiet part out loud—the part that Baum, McPherson, and Orfield cannot bring themselves to say even today. The argument of his Howard speech is the only coherent theory of civil rights: if no racial group is innately inferior to another and opportunity is genuinely equally distributed, then we should expect to see equal outcomes across groups. The upshot is that if a social system is producing unequal group outcomes, the only reasonable conclusion is that opportunities are not distributed equally. This is what Johnson was saying. It is what the Black Power movement was saying. And it is what Martin Luther King, Jr., was saying with increasing vehemence from 1965 through 1968 as Johnson and the Democratic Party got cold feet.

The quiet part generally went quiet again as liberals and progressives tried to preserve and extend civil rights gains in the face of vigorous white opposition. But equality is the civil rights logic that any accurate analysis of educational outcomes must reckon with, even while acknowledging the successes and likelihood of backlash. Equal opportunity and equal outcomes are not the same concept, but they are inevitably connected, and the connection was always in view during the height of civil rights enforcement.

On this point, Baum, McPherson, and Orfield put themselves in an awkward position. All three authors are distraught at our "age of inequality." The main point of both books is to show how higher education has become utterly hamstrung by rampant inequality in every other sphere of life. Most of Baum and McPherson's chapters discuss pre-college forms of inequality that pervade the lives of working-class students and students of color. Orfield lists the "racial inequalities that often severely limit the development of students of color on the path to college," identifying twenty-two distinct, damaging items—from growing up in homes where reduced resources have reduced their learning before they start school, to experiencing residential isolation from strong schools and districts, to having more residential instability, to being more liable to suspension and school policing, to having fewer teachers of their own race and ethnicity, to having less information about college, and so on. Both books offer accurate, convincing portraits of racial equality in a long retreat.

But both books stop short of drawing the obvious moral: that American education is trapped in an inequality machine—what other authors forthrightly call racial capitalism—and that rather than continuing to fall in line, it must stop complying and reinvent civil rights from the ground up. In fact, Orfield calls Johnson's vision of equal outcomes an "outlier," marginalizing it early on in his book. Baum and McPherson call for better pathways to degree completion, better advising, and more auditing of colleges to improve "accountability." We've long been doing the last of these, to little effect, and the authors give no reason why their other prescriptions will do much better.

Baum and McPherson do say we need to focus on "reducing the differences in opportunities and outcomes between individuals from low-income backgrounds and those with more resources." Yes—but that's where the book should *start*, not where it should end! They add, "There is persuasive evidence that spending more on the education" of students at community colleges and other broad-access institutions "pays off in higher graduation rates." Yes! So let's spend more—a lot more! "Inadequate funding of broad-access colleges is a major national problem." Yes! So let's actually fund the reduction of racialized outcomes gaps! These sentences appear on page 198 of a 264-page book, effectively dissolved in a reservoir of anxiety about costs. The glimmers of a new dawn for funding are lost in Republican-style bootstrapping claims that even poor colleges can do much better "with the scant resources that many of these institutions have."

Orfield, for his part, calls for "race-sensitive" policies and wants to tear down the "walls" of unequal school preparation and inade-quate college financial aid. But he offers no major investment plans that would actually do this, and his biggest wall is his own worry about public expense. (One bit of good news is that the social costs of equalized education have been greatly exaggerated. A group in California calculated the cost to the median taxpayer of creating free college for all three of that state's public systems, with state funding raised back to inflation-adjusted 2001 levels, would have cost the median worker, in 2018, an additional $66 per year.)

The pattern is pervasive. Both books are preoccupied with targeting programs rather than generalizing them. This is the longtime Clinton-Obama strategy that has undermined political solidarity, eroded the philosophy of social goods required by all, and insured uneven results. Both books reject the two most significant educational social movements of the past decades—the movement for free college and the movement for student debt cancellation—that have driven a renaissance of race-conscious analysis of disparate impacts. And both books focus on increasing limited kinds of procedural fairness, clouding the egalitarian vision animating the overall struggle.

The result—like so much cognitive dissonance in a mind divided against itself—makes for painful reading. "I'm not a neoliberal," the ego insists, but the superego plainly is. This split creates the limbo in which so much progressive policy thinking finds itself today. These authors know that post-*Brown* education policies have failed, generating inequality by their very nature. And the authors are opposed to current levels of inequality. But they cannot muster the political will or directly summon the intellectual resources to challenge an inherently anti-egalitarian system. Instead, they invite us to go on "tinkering toward utopia," as two historians of school reform put it in a different context more than twenty years ago.

Newfield

In reality, the portrait of inequality so scrupulously depicted in these books implies a conclusion their authors effectively recoil from: that we must massively rebuild a full range of social systems on truly egalitarian grounds. In practice, this means using the general tax system, not the selective tuition system, to support general, high-quality, equitably distributed educational resources accessible to all. It means highly progressive tax rates on income, wealth, and financial transactions of various kinds. It means redirecting money away from the places where resources have disproportionately and unfairly pooled during the past four decades, into neighborhoods, regions, and districts that have been unjustly neglected. It means building affordable housing for students and their families, guaranteeing health and child care and good jobs, and transforming community safety. And through it all, it means repudiating the neoliberal deference to markets and reviving a forceful role for government in securing the public good.

In short, we need nothing less than a comprehensive reconstruction of U.S. society. As these books themselves make so clear, the roots of educational injustice extend far beyond classroom walls and school district boundaries. Better academic mentoring, a strong program of affirmative action, and "feasible" adjustments in district funding will never cut it on their own; they are at best Band-Aids laid over the critical wounds of racial capitalism. The reason the problem will never be solved solely by changes at the level of individual educational institutions—or even under the isolated rubric of "education policy" writ large—is that the problem is the whole interlocking structure of social and economic life in which our educational institutions are embedded. It will take more than Baum and McPherson's passing reference to this fact to meet this challenge.

This vision—a massive program of just distribution across all the core areas of U.S. society, administered by the full force and effect of the developmental welfare state—is a functionally socialist project from the vantage of mainstream U.S. politics today. Perhaps this is why the very idea is unspeakable in nearly all education policy discussions in the United States: afraid to sound "political" (much less socialist), they aspire to be neutrally technocratic. Yet nothing in these books—or their many similar kin—suggests any *other* way to get equal educational outcomes of the kind justice requires; we have already endlessly tried. There is no escaping the fact that equality of outcome must be a substantive political goal. The conclusion these books force on us, however indirectly, is that we must take it seriously.

THE EARTH FOR MAN
Jo Guldi

IN 1951 officers of the United Nations' Food and Agriculture Organization (FAO) gathered in Rome to contemplate their founders' mission: to serve the decolonizing nations of the world by helping peasant farmers maintain control over their own land. That same year, the organization had relocated away from its previous headquarters in Washington, D.C. It was a move away from the halls of power, but toward the emerging power centers of New Delhi, Cairo, Moscow, Beijing, Jakarta, and Manila—and symbolically, at least, toward Mexico City, Santiago, Antigua, and Lima.

Eight years earlier international delegates had assembled in Hot Springs, Virginia, to spell out the work of the future United Nations. British, American, and Indian soldiers were clashing with the soldiers of the Third Reich, which embraced the philosophy of *lebensraum*, or "living space"—the conceit that a growing German population would require more land, the subjugation of other peoples, and the creation of farms in colonized territory where German peasants would settle.

Meanwhile, millions of Bengalis were starving in the latest of the famines that had plagued the subcontinent under British rule; up to three million perished in 1943.

Franklin Roosevelt had recently declared a worldwide "freedom from want" as an American value, and the designers of the United Nations would try to imagine a world of plenty, where Indians ate as well as Britons—even if it meant that Britons would be required to make sacrifices. Indeed, advocates of redistribution at the UN's FAO would labor to create something unique in history to sustain that vision: an international organization largely concerned with land, invested with an unprecedented power to advise governments around the world and with the authority to construct grand plans for centering land as a resource for the world's people. Embodying this remarkable mandate, the FAO was given the Latin motto *Fiat Panis*, or "Let There Be Bread."

What made such a radical conversation possible? Many of the delegates who congregated in the 1943 FAO Quebec conferences had participated in a wide-ranging wartime debate in Britain about hunger, agriculture, racism, and opportunity. Social scientists such as Doreen Warriner argued that political stability would emerge only when empires agreed to surrender their land. Warriner and her colleagues would spend the years immediately after the war pressing for a global government of land; the FAO enshrined their ideas. At the time, China's Communist Party had already begun an era of land redistribution focused on creating family farms; Guatemala and Egypt would soon pass land redistribution schemes modeled on those in Ireland, whereby landlords would be compensated for land turned over to peasant farmers.

Guldi

Because of the UN's obligation to support member nations in the developing world, administrators at the FAO based their strategy on the historical arc of peasant struggles for territory, not on a commitment to capitalism, economic growth, or some other abstraction (even while those abstractions sometimes entered discussions about the consequences of land redistribution). Later the Washington Consensus would dominate world affairs, but in 1951 the conversation that mattered most in many parts of the world was taking shape in Rome.

To many midcentury observers, world events since 1881—from the rent strikes and related events in Ireland, India, and Britain, and their corollaries in Mexico, Asia, Africa, and Eastern Europe—had united the distant corners of the decaying British Empire into a single march for justice. There had been peasant uprisings in Mexico and the rest of Latin America, where peasant-led rebellions turned over haciendas—the colonial ranches of the aristocracy—to indigenous peoples and rural laborers; in the Philippines, where the United States presided over a land redistribution to break up ancient estates and create small plots of land; in Soviet Russia, where the state seized large and medium-scale farms in the name of the peasant; and in Taiwan, Japan, and countless other nations.

Land redistribution was a central focus of peasant movements in Ireland, India, and other places where racial underclasses had been denied the possibility of owning land for centuries, laboring as underpaid, uneducated tenants or sharecroppers. Wherever these movements erupted into organized revolutions, redistribution of land was a primary demand. If decolonization succeeded, the descendants of enslaved persons and sharecroppers and tenants might thus become landowners in their own right.

Administrators at the FAO came to believe that their institution might guide the coming revolution in land toward the most efficient and rational outcome possible. In their view, the FAO would house a new kind of bureaucracy—an international government charged with challenging the traditional elites of the world. Civil servants and social scientists would become the servants of peasant revolution.

WHEN the FAO's Edmundo Flores visited farmers in a remote village in the Bolivian Andes in 1952, he found peasants there quoting the slogans associated with Mexico: "Viva Zapata! Land and Freedom! Death to the landlords!" At first, Flores thought the slogans were evidence of Marxism, but eventually, he discovered another answer: tiny movie houses had started up in the villages, and among the favorite films were Hollywood reels that retold the story of the Mexican Revolution. Cast in the role of Emiliano Zapata, Marlon Brando took up the cause of the native rights that should have belonged to peasants, battling evil landlords along the way.

Just as newspapers and ballads had spread stories of the Irish land reform to North America and Australia a generation before, cinema conveyed the legend of the Mexican Revolution across Latin America. Whether amplified by film, oral tradition, or literature, the slogan "Land to the Tiller" soon spread not only to Bolivia but even to Honduras, Colombia, and Peru.

Guldi

Carried on this wave, global redistribution of land seemed inevitable to many observers in the 1940s and '50s. As movies began broadcasting the message of a right to occupation around the globe, Flores concluded that the fictionalized depictions of Mexico's revolutionary peasants, male and female alike, "convey more of a message than, say, the Communist Manifesto ever has."

Flores's observation was particularly cutting, in retrospect, as it voiced his conviction that land reform was a force that worked in *opposition* to communism: peasants would not need to create a dictatorship of the proletariat, he suggested, if democratic movements were able to redistribute land and thereby create a fairer economy.

Flores was not alone in this observation. A broad consensus in North America and Europe held that land redistribution was inevitable; the only question was whether the program executed would be capitalist or communist in nature. British social scientists, steeped in the history of enclosure of common land, were soon called upon to develop a theoretical framework encompassing the postcolonial condition and to construct an international institution charged with fighting hunger in the developing world. Many of the theories emphasized the reality and inevitability of peasant revolution around the globe.

The elaboration of these theories owes a great deal to Warriner. The daughter of a Staffordshire farmer and granddaughter of an exiled Irish radical, Warriner earned her PhD specializing in the transitions in Eastern Europe, the site of both peaceful and violent land turnovers. She started teaching at the University of London, but in 1938, as news of Chamberlain's accommodation of Hitler reached London, she turned down a prestigious fellowship in the United States and instead flew to Prague, where she had researched peasant agriculture eight years before. There, she began to learn the stories—social democratic leaders being sent to concentration camps, Jewish families disappearing—that had not yet reached the West. As the war raged on, Warriner organized camps and trains for a thousand working-class anti-Nazi dissenters and Jewish families and coordinated safe transport for them to Canada, where they could settle as farmers on small plots of land.

Returning home after the war, Warriner joined forces with Paul Lamartine Yates, author of a study of food production in six European nations. One of Yates's first appointments was as a junior member of Seebohm Rowntree's committee on British agriculture, which published a 1938 report revealing a systematic relationship between poverty, underconsumption of food, and ill health, and prescribed a mandate for the state to direct food production and remedy the conditions of workers.

A decade later found Yates writing about agriculture with Warriner, then joining other experts on nutrition to found the FAO. Warriner and Yates felt certain that the major challenge ahead was in transforming the plight of impoverished peasants around the world: a population that, like the peasants of Eastern Europe, had only undergone a "very recent emancipation from serfdom."

Warriner argued that small farms could offer a sustainable life for political and ethnic refugees like those she had helped in Prague. She also believed that land reform more generally offered a path to democratic prosperity: in her many books on the topic,

Warriner regularly invoked the family farm systems of the United States, Canada, New Zealand, and Australia as evidence that land settlement created stable democracies.

To Warriner and Yates, the rise of authoritarian governments represented a clear threat to these objectives. Reflecting on recent clashes in Eastern Europe, they warned that land redistribution, while ameliorating the economic burden of the peasants, might be used to impose authoritarian rule—as it had in the Soviet Union and its satellites. Such initiatives could thus facilitate the rise of "military cliques and semi-fascist dictatorships."

What was needed, then, was not merely land redistribution but also economic independence, such that farmers could actively engage and defend a democracy that reflected the range of their interests. To avoid authoritarian control, new states would need to create opportunity rapidly, and this required economic planning—especially the coordination of prices and markets and programs to teach peasants about technology. Warriner and Yates recommended a system of cooperatives and shared technology supporting small, economically independent farmers who could then make up their own minds about politics. Such plans would provide new states with comprehensive economic programs for both cities and towns, ensuring the "economic conditions under which the peasants can greatly increase their outputs," and that both urban and rural workers could look for "a steadily rising level of incomes."

Warriner and Yates theorized that planned economies were most vital for rural workers due to the nature of the agricultural cycle. Peasants, they argued, were economically vulnerable in an industrial economy where workers with wage increases were likely to spend more of their money on manufactured goods than on food. Modern states could cushion peasants from the inherent vulnerability of agricultural enterprise, which, unlike manufacturing, couldn't be planned several months or even years in advance and couldn't be easily scaled to adjust to new information from the market.

State programs could ameliorate human misery, they argued, and governments should adopt measures to protect agricultural workers; such sound engagements, they reasoned, could inoculate peasants against the political promises offered by would-be despots. They wrote: "Man is beginning to realize that he can exercise control. . . . Peasants in their economic lives are still at the mercy of the rest of the community which exploits them, but this state of affairs need not continue for ever." Coordinated expenditure and management by a centralized bureaucratic state could enable a new economy—one marked by "economic conditions under which the peasants can greatly increase their output," even supplying a "steadily rising level of incomes."

Economic planning thus lay at the root of a general revolution to increase prosperity and economic security while ensuring a path to democracy in which peasants would not be easily wooed by authoritarian forces. According to Warriner and Yates, by setting farmers up with individual plots of soil, land redistribution would be a key element of economic planning in most nations. In a later book published in 1955, Warriner laid out a plan premised on recent UN reports that, in her words, "put forward the contention that land reform . . . must be regarded as a condition of economic development." Soon after describing these schemes in print, Warriner and Yates would each have opportunities to realize them. While Warriner went on to advise a variety of postcolonial nations, Yates would help to found the FAO, working alongside John Boyd Orr, another veteran of the British crusade against hunger.

Unlike Yates the activist, Orr was a professor turned adviser to the state. Experiments published by Orr in 1927 proved that Scottish schoolchildren given milk grew stronger than their peers. He was the veteran of a campaign to remedy the condition of Britain's working classes by providing cheap access to food. His 1936 report, *Food, Health, and Income*, argued for an increased role by the state in the nutrition of the poor. In the decade that followed, Europe was wracked by food shortages, and Orr's work offered a model for European policy.

In 1945 Orr appeared in Quebec at the FAO conference as an unofficial adviser. Despite having been excluded from the official British delegation, Orr electrified the conference with a sermon in which he condemned political inaction about nutrition in vivid terms. "The people wanted bread," said Orr, "but were given statistics." The next year, Orr was selected as the FAO's first director general.

Orr, like Yates and Warriner, believed that state planning could level human disparities. Orr had already spent a decade publishing books that envisioned a top-down food board for Britain that would collect information on where food was grown and where it could be sold and then advise farmers about what to grow. At the FAO, Orr would style the same dreams on a global scale. Orr's agenda was threefold: establishing the FAO as an independent, policymaking institution capable of recommending global strategies; combating the worst consequences of poverty by supporting a worldwide food program (a "World Food Plan"); and challenging the long-term consequences of racism in Europe's former colonies.

Orr's view of how a coordinating institution could support society was, if anything, even grander than that of Warriner and Yates. He wished to level the short divide not merely between rich and poor or rural and urban, but also between different races and different experiences of empire.

Addressing the fate of former colonies in the postwar world, Orr recast a phrase that Kipling had used in a very different sense when complaining of the "White Man's Burden" to educate and civilize the "backward" races of the world through violence and conquest. Orr's 1953 book *The White Man's Dilemma* warned of the widening gulf between the "haves" and "have-nots" would "end in holocaust" unless a "world authority" provided "environmental conditions which would enable [the poor] to attain their full inherited capacity for physical and mental ability." Such a world authority, he argued, would effectively eliminate all "difference between the ability of men of different races."

Orr's prophecy bears quoting at length:

> The natives of Asia, Africa, and Latin America would become the equals of the white man, and as these continents became industrialized the Europeans and their descendants, the Americans, would lose the control of the world they gained in their 300 years of conquest from the seventeenth to the nineteenth centuries. This, then, is the white man's dilemma. He can attempt by force to maintain military and economic supremacy . . . the final outcome of which will be the downfall of Western civilization. On the other hand, he can . . . join

the human family and use his present industrial supremacy to develop the resources of the earth to put an end to hunger and poverty, with resulting world-wide economic prosperity.

Worldwide flourishing, Orr suggested, would require hard choices by rich nations and individuals; only visionary sacrifice could support the infrastructure required to prevent violent confrontations for generations to come. He coyly alluded to sacrifices in his book, but as the work of others at the FAO made clear, the primary sacrifice was for whites to give up their claim to land.

Although largely forgotten today, Orr's work embodied an impressive optimism regarding the potential of social science and international governance to remedy long-term inequalities on a global scale. For his advocacy of a "world food plan" and his work to create the FAO, Orr received the 1949 Nobel Peace Prize.

Working alongside Yates and Orr was Frank Lidgett McDougall, a rugged Australian settler turned seasoned diplomat. In his youth, McDougall claimed, he cleared eighty acres to plant fruit trees before joining the Australian agricultural lobby in London as it negotiated for preferential trade terms with Britain and the outside world. He considered himself an "artist at propaganda," and he was described by his contemporaries as a master statesman, skilled at concealing his agenda while he brought others on board.

If Orr and Yates were civil servants with an activist streak, McDougall's credentials were capitalistic and pragmatic. They were all inspired by discoveries in the relatively young science of nutrition, but where Orr and Yates saw opportunities for state reform to relieve the poor, for McDougall, the discovery of undernourished populations and concerned governments in Europe meant promising new markets for Australian produce. McDougall also understood firsthand how a former colony might struggle for fair terms of trade. He offered a capitalist perspective that overlapped with an anticolonial one: What opportunities, McDougall asked, might science open up for former colonies under a new world order?

Despite the FAO's founders' anti-racism and anticolonialism, we should not lose sight of their own racial privilege. As white men who were British citizens or subjects, they enjoyed advantages that many of their colonial counterparts did not. Yet Orr's anti-racism was distinctly ahead of its time, standing in direct contrast to the prognostications of contemporaries such as John Russell—the former director of Britain's Rothamsted Experimental Station, the country's major center for agricultural research. Orr was an exception in the husk of the British Empire, where the legacy of racial injustice was still abundantly clear to anyone who looked.

For the most part, British administrators, still clinging to empire, were terrified of the conversations happening elsewhere. In 1952, Kenya's British administrators learned of native movements to reclaim the traditional landholdings on which the Kikuyu people were now nominally "squatters" on white-owned farms. They rounded up the Kikuyu into concentration camps, tortured and massacred them, and summarily suppressed evidence of the atrocities. In South Africa, Australia, the United States and many other countries, white-run governments tyrannized natives and minorities; land redistribution remained a subject beyond debate.

Despite such resistance, Yates, Orr, and McDougall formed the lobby at the Homestead Hotel in Hot Springs, Virginia, in 1943—

well before the United Nations officially formed—that persuaded the gathered nations of the benefits of possible cooperation around agriculture. Their privilege was matched with opportunism. A year later McDougall proposed "an international agency for food and agriculture" as a UN activity that would be bold in intent, but realistic in terms of diplomacy—"not too controversial." Further diplomacy gained the agency a budget—almost one-third of which was supported by the United States—a headquarters, a staff, and a growing mandate to solve the potential troubles of nutrition, population, and agriculture associated with the developing world.

The FAO would become the global institutional pivot of ideas about land redistribution and postcolonial emancipation. It was not as powerful as some would have liked, but it was a government all the same, charged with reconfiguring the map of inequality around the world.

WHEN FORMER COLONIES declared their independence from Europe, many were largely composed of impoverished agrarian populations still reeling from decades of endemic famines and droughts. The chief weapon of extortion under most European empires had been colonial landholding, and most former colonies wanted to undo the consolidation of landownership in the hands of a few wealthy absentees; a majority of the population tilled the soil in abject poverty so that Europeans abroad could enjoy the profits of colonized labor. Entire infrastructures concentrated on exporting food from starving nations rather than feeding poor farmers when droughts hit. Some nations proposed a suite of reforms. For instance, India insisted that any new international agreements must work to reverse the sins of empire.

In 1943 an interim committee discussed the possibility of exporting food from rich nations to famished ones as part of the FAO agenda. The debate reflected some representatives' concern for protecting markets for rich nations. But relieving Bengal's famine remained a subject of earnest attention, as did the issue of fair representation for poorer nations. And, as the United Nations took form, an ideal of fairness—one nation, one vote—gave the former colonies voice. The program for managing the world supply of food did not simply fall to the developed world. Much of the FAO's agenda would be shaped by the former colonies, and the postcolonial nations themselves would demand the FAO's commitment to land redistribution.

As early as 1948 the FAO's second director general, Norris Dodd, embarked on a tour of India where he met with Indian economists whose ideas would be interwoven into policy at the FAO. In particular, their research helped direct FAO policy objectives toward minimizing developing world debt and prioritizing economic development on terms dictated by the developing world. FAO agents would thus digest and reformulate a strategy for land redistribution around the globe. Deferring to member nations in the postcolonial and developing world, the FAO's agenda focused not simply on food markets but also on justice.

In 1951 Dodd gave a speech to the Federal Council of Churches. He compared slogans that had defined Germany and Poland as territories for the "master race" to the U.S.'s own anti-immigrant campaign, "America for Americans." Dodd proposed a "uniting" values system instead, summed up by the title of his speech: "The Earth for Man." Dodd's slogan signaled the FAO's commitment to combating hunger, disease, and poverty—the same values that President Truman had defined as central to U.S. ambitions in his "Point Four" speech three years earlier. Dodd recast Truman's fight against poverty in materialist and ecological terms: "Can we use the resources of the earth well enough so that all people everywhere can have, or see clear hope for, a decent life?" The FAO's mission, Dodd indicated, was to encourage the nations of the world to deploy knowledge, technology, and policy to prevent exclusion and exploitation.

Redistributive justice remained at the forefront of the FAO's agenda for at least its first ten years. In 1953 Dodd addressed a conference of the leaders of young persons' movements, who gathered in Rome under the aegis of the World Assembly of Youth. Dodd put the issue of land distribution front and center. "In many countries the land-owning, land-holding, land-renting laws and customs do not provide the farmer with security of tenure on his land," he declared. Dodd articulated a plan for land redistribution that involved rethinking landlord and tenant relationships. "These laws and customs cannot very well be changed—even slowly and carefully as they should be, in accord with the traditions of the country—unless people also come to understand and agree with the changes that should be made," he explained.

The land redistribution agenda shaped the general organization of the FAO down to the directives handed to individual agents. A major 1951 FAO report had laid out a roadmap for global economic development and food production, targeting land monopoly as a subject for reform: both holdings that were too vast—and therefore wasteful—and holdings too small for subsistence agriculture should be targeted and reformed. Both represented a residue of colonialism, according to the report, that needed reform. Single-owner proprietors must be supported by an array of state provisions of institutional infrastructure, including secure land tenure policies, freedom from eviction, the titling of owned land, and credit at reasonable rates. The FAO would target the redistribution of land from large landholders to smallholders as the most effective policy for states to pursue economic growth while developing a political environment suited to democracy.

The 1951 report also directly responded to the demands of developing nations. Here the FAO explicitly pledged to undertake the creation of regional centers in Brazil, Thailand, and Iraq to concentrate on land problems. To accommodate an expanding list of client states pursuing land redistribution and related programs, the FAO would have to form new administrative branches. Later that same year, as it relocated from Washington to Rome, it received funding for a new technical wing, the Agriculture Division, which encompassed several "branches": Animal Production, Plant Production, Land and Water Use, Rural Welfare, and Agricultural Institutions and Services.

Throughout most of the 1950s and '60s, the FAO's agenda aligned with policy ideas in Britain and the United States. American policies and land redistribution programs, for example, in Japan, Taiwan, the Philippines, and Latin America were compatible with ideas at the FAO, and reflected the earlier ideas of Warriner, Yates, Orr, and Dodd. Throughout these decades, the U.S. Department of State sponsored international conferences on agriculture stressing land redistribution as a key component of international development. In 1961, in sympathy with Kennedy's Alliance for Progress, Latin American countries vowed, in the Declaration of Punta del Este, to encourage "programs of comprehensive agrarian reform." This easy alignment, however, was not destined to last. The United States began to pursue a fundamentally different vision of rural development—one aligned more with elite interests than with the ideas emerging in the developing world.

Moreover, the FAO's effectiveness would be limited by the organization's ability to navigate a tension among the United Nations' member nations. While the leading powers of Europe and America relinquished a measure of control to the votes of newly independent nations, they remained chary of giving up control over sovereignty issues. Like the League of Nations before it, the United Nations' role was defined, therefore, as an "advisory" body. No UN branches had the power to compel. The FAO, therefore, was charged with merely advising member nations in developing their own ministries of agriculture and their own agricultural policies.

BY THE 1970s, the Rome Consensus had forged a fully developed ideology for a global economy in which the small farmers of the developing world could flourish. The tenets of this consensus required the nations of the world to recognize the importance of protecting the beneficiaries of land reform from local elites, the potential power of cooperative networks to supply small farmers with technology and infrastructure, and the value of participatory democracy. This utopian set of ideas informed a growing bureaucracy of agrarian experts, surveyors, cartographers, and policy analysts whose influence, even while it fluctuated in the United States, was aligned both with Rome and with a broadening swath of decolonizing nations abroad.

Indeed, the ideas themselves emerged partly from the dreams of Europe and partly from the disgust of peasants around the world—sick with the poverty bequeathed them by empire, they demanded equal access to the earth. It emerged partly also from the worldviews of social scientists, many directly connected to the fight against Nazi Germany, who looked to small farms as a source of sustainable economies.

The hopes for a global revolution in land redistribution rested, at the international level, on one primary institutional strategy: the work of the United Nations would provide a forum for solving the problems of developing nations. With the help of this institution, a new elite, charged with Weberian ideas of duty and rationalization, would challenge the traditional power of empire or race. Bureaucracy was thus key to the envisioned revolution. Effective land redistribution would depend on the agitation of civil servants, government experts, and popular leaders who understood themselves to be servants of peasant and popular rebellions against oppression. A new elite of educated social scientists would lead the way toward peasant liberation around the world.

But it was not Warriner and the FAO's theory of decolonization that dominated in Washington, where a slate of Ivy

League professors began to preach a "modernization" theory that framed economic growth as the ultimate virtue. In the Washington Consensus that emerged later, far away from Rome, global hopes about the development of poorer counties were increasingly articulated not in terms of justice but rather in terms of consumption. As Wolfgang Sachs observed of the outlook for development in 1992, "Across the world hopes for the future are fixed on the rich man's patterns of production and consumption."

Many individuals would look to markets, rather than states, as an avenue for implementing social policy. The era saw a massive counterreaction against modern bureaucracy that grew out of a broader conservative movement against the state. Neoliberals attacked the "red tape" of modern government. They argued that market exchanges represented a more rational approach to modeling human society, as distinct from the oppressive and irrational management of the state. A new era was marked by government from the "private" sphere, characterized by the expanding presence of NGOs in every initiative connected to development and poverty. As prominent voices in the United States began to target the spread of communism worldwide, many began to attack land redistribution as a form of communism in disguise. With the withdrawal of U.S. support, the brave visions that had emerged at the FAO began to founder.

However we may assess the United Nations, many of us now share a view of history in which the theft of land from indigenous people is central to the transformations of capitalism and states over the last several hundred years. Such an understanding may drive us to wonder about possible remedies for the mass evictions of the past and further possible displacements in the future. Could coordinated land redistribution programs or rent controls today make homes for those displaced by flood, fire, drought, and famine?

THE FALSE PROMISE OF OPPORTUNITY ZONES

Timothy Weaver

IN JUNE 2020 Donald Trump tweeted, in characteristically hyperbolic style, that his administration had "done more for the Black Community than any President since Abraham Lincoln." First in the list of his putative achievements were Opportunity Zones (OZs), a stealthy provision of the Tax Cuts and Jobs Act of 2017 that offers capital gains tax reductions in the name of incentivizing investment in "low-income" regions and "distressed communities."

At a number of rallies that summer, Trump went on to claim—without evidence—that thanks to OZs, "countless jobs and $100 billion of new investment . . . have poured into 9,000 of our most distressed neighborhoods anywhere in the country." (Estimates of the actual amount of investment are lower.) Trump also lauded the program in his State of the Union address earlier that year, claiming that "wealthy people and companies are pouring money into poor neighborhoods or areas that haven't seen investment in many decades, creating jobs, energy, and excitement. This is the first time that these deserving communities have seen anything like this."

The OZ initiative starts from the premise that communities are distressed because of a lack of private investment and that tax policy offers an easy solution. As the Economic Innovation Group (EIG)—a think tank established in 2013 to promote this view—puts it, "the tax code should encourage private investment in communities that are struggling to attract capital, create jobs, and lift residents out of poverty." The incentive under the Trump tax bill applies to taxpayers who make a qualified investment in a Qualified Opportunity Fund (QOF), which in turn must invest at least 90 percent of its assets in a designated OZ. QOFs operate as investment vehicles, organized as corporations or partnerships. A variety of entities have established or invested in QOFs, including real estate private equity firms, investment banks, supermarket chains, and hedge funds. To qualify as an OZ, a census tract must be either a low-income community—with a poverty rate of at least 20 percent, or a median family income of no greater than 80 percent of the state's median income—or contiguous to one. States could nominate up to 25 percent of their low-income communities, and the year after the bill became law, U.S. Treasury officials certified 8,764 nominations, amounting to about 10 percent of all tracts in the United States.

There are three key tax advantages associated with the program. First, investors can defer paying taxes until the end of 2026 if they place capital gains they have realized elsewhere into a QOF—amounting, in effect, to an interest-free loan. Second, taxes on those gains are reduced depending on how long investors keep their assets in a QOF:

10 percent for five years, 15 percent for seven years. Third, investors can avoid paying any capital gains taxes whatsoever on gains that are realized from the QOF itself if the investment is held for a decade.

The scheme may sound attractive: What could be so bad about giving the wealthy an incentive to pour money into impoverished neighborhoods? But contrary to Trump's breathless claims, a mounting body of evidence shows that OZs simply don't work—at least if the goal is to help lift low-income communities out of poverty rather than redistribute wealth upward, subsidize luxury real estate development, and facilitate gentrification.

In fact, the idea that tax breaks can help revitalize distressed communities has a long history, one that stretches back to the early days of the neoliberal revolution in the United Kingdom. The scheme was imported to the United States by conservatives and eventually won bipartisan support in the 1990s, but the strategy didn't work in the UK, and it hasn't worked here. Contrary to the hopes of the Biden administration and a bipartisan group of reformers in Congress, Trump's overly lax program cannot be salvaged with better reporting and oversight. Addressing place-based deprivation requires a different approach altogether—one that empowers communities and local governments rather than seeks to court private investors.

THE PROXIMATE ORIGINS of OZs can be traced to billionaire Sean Parker—Napster cofounder, the first president of Facebook, and a former board member of Spotify. As Parker explained in 2018, he wanted to find ways to encourage investors to channel capital gains into run-down areas. "People were sitting on large capital gains with low basis and huge appreciation," he said. "There was all this money sitting on the sidelines. . . I started thinking: How do we get investors to put money into places where they wouldn't normally invest?"

As journalist David Wessel vividly details in his book *Only the Rich Can Play* (2021), Parker along with fellow investors used $8.5 million to bankroll EIG and recruited bipartisan leadership. Steve Glickman, a former senior advisor to President Barack Obama, and John Lettieri, former aide to Republican Senator Chuck Hagel, joined Parker as cofounders, while Kevin Hassett, Trump's chief economist, and Jared Bernstein, who held the same position for then-Vice President Joe Biden, served on the economic advisory board. (Bernstein has since joined Biden's Council of Economic Advisers; Biden recently nominated him to be its chair.)

In 2015 Hassett and Bernstein wrote an EIG brief outlining key underpinnings of the OZ idea. Noting that "a very large stock of savings in the form of unrealized capital gains has built up in recent years," they called for incentives that would establish "a new equilibrium where investors flock to distressed areas because they are confident that other investors will as well, then the investments will also have the potential to be highly profitable, which would feed a virtuous cycle." Such a program, they argued, would "partially address widening inequality and lack of economic mobility in targeted areas, but do so in a manner that relies on markets and new enterprise to help the poor."

A legislative breakthrough came when Senators Tim Scott (Republican of South Carolina) and Cory Booker (Democrat of New

Jersey) drafted the Investing in Opportunity Act in early 2017, but despite the bill's fourteen cosponsors in the Senate, House Speaker Paul Ryan had doubts. Trump, too, had little interest at first, but things changed after his incendiary remarks about a white nationalist protest in Charlottesville in the summer of 2017. According to Wessel, Scott met with Trump and urged him to help undo the PR damage by backing OZs. With Trump onboard, Ryan's opposition faded, and the bill was inserted into the reconciliation bill that won congressional approval in December 2017.

Far from a truly innovative program, however, opportunity zones are an old idea—and the history tells a cautionary tale. The basic idea first emerged in the UK in the 1970s amid serious concerns about the deterioration of British inner cities. The devastating effects of deindustrialization were compounded by the stagflation that bedeviled both left and right governments since the late 1960s. It was in this context that urbanists and politicians cast about for alternatives to Keynesianism.

One proposal came from Sir Peter Hall, a geographer by training, who lamented the moribund state of Britain's great cities. In a 1977 speech to the Royal Town Planning Institute, Hall argued that the revival of urban areas required a dose of "fairly shameless free enterprise." Inspired by the meteoric rise of cities like Hong Kong and Singapore, Hall's "freeport solution" envisaged "free zones," which would lie "outside the limits of the parent country's legislation"—free from taxes and regulations and where "bureaucracy would be kept to an absolute minimum." As Hall later acknowledged, the speech reflected his "blue sky" thinking and was made "slightly tongue in cheek." As such, he "did not expect anyone to take this seriously in policy terms." He was therefore very surprised to receive a call from Geoffrey Howe inviting him to lunch.

Unlike Hall, who hailed from the left, Howe was a key member of Margaret Thatcher's Conservative Party shadow cabinet. Once he became chancellor of the Exchequer in 1979, Howe launched a neoliberal transformation in British economic policymaking with the introduction of monetarism, tax cuts, and deregulation. What united Hall and Howe was their common concern with urban woes and a shared commitment to using neoliberal techniques to ameliorate them. Although Howe was concerned about British cities in general, he was especially keen to arrest the decline of London's docks. Indeed, Howe chose the Waterman's Arms—a pub on the Isle of Dogs in the heart of what became known as Docklands—to give a "major speech" in 1978 on the deleterious state of British cities. As he puts it: "There, in the midst of dockland dereliction at its most depressing, I launched the idea of Enterprise Zones."

In a classic statement of what would become neoliberal orthodoxy across the globe, Howe blamed regulation and taxation for Docklands' decline, arguing that the region's "urban wilderness" represented the "developing sickness of our society" in which "the burgeoning of State activity now positively frustrates healthy, private initiative, widely dispersed and properly rewarded." For Howe, the "frustrating domination of widespread public land ownership and public intervention into virtually all private activities has produced a form of municipal mortmain which will not be shifted without a huge effort of will."

Weaver

In Howe's view, the only cures were to be found in "fundamental reform of our tax system"—he meant tax cuts—and "the sensible deregulation of our economy." And while Howe (like Thatcher) sought to apply this formula for the British economy writ large, he recognized that it would take time to accumulate the necessary political capital to transform the entire British economy in the neoliberal image. Still, in Docklands he saw a unique opportunity for a quicker transformation. Enterprise zones, as he put it, would "go further and more swiftly than the general policy changes that we have been proposing to liberate enterprise throughout the country. . . . the idea would be to set up test market areas or laboratories in which to enable fresh policies to prime the pump of prosperity, and to establish their potential for doing so elsewhere." The introduction of enterprise zones was not only a way of "trying out our ideas," Howe thought, but also a "kind of trial run intended to foster support for the other possible changes, which we sought to introduce more broadly in the British economy."

Having convinced Thatcher of the efficacy of enterprise zones, Howe included them in his 1980 budget "with the intention that each of them should be developed with as much freedom as possible for those who work there to make profits and to create jobs." Ultimately the conservatives enacted eleven enterprise zones, with the most prominent located in the Isle of Dogs. Besides enjoying 100 percent capital allowances for both industrial and commercial buildings—meaning that the total costs of new buildings could be deducted from taxable profits—companies in the zones would see complete relief from development land taxes, ratings, industrial training certificates, and levies and a drastically simplified planning scheme.

THE IDEA would not stay put. Across the Atlantic, enterprise zones soon caught the attention of Stuart Butler of the Heritage Foundation and Congressman Jack Kemp, Republican of New York who championed Ronald Reagan's tax-cutting agenda.

Butler thought the causes of urban decay in the UK and the United States were "sufficiently similar to allow possible solutions voiced in Britain to be given serious consideration in the United States." He concluded that enterprise zones would go some way toward solving the "urban crisis" that plagued U.S. cities. His conviction was that slashing taxes—and, where possible, regulations—would encourage the development of small business, which he viewed as critical for urban revival. For his part, Kemp—like Hall and Howe—was inspired by the rise of Hong Kong, which he characterized as "free-trade zone, free-banking zone and a free-enterprise zone." The key to emulating Hong Kong's apparent success, Kemp thought, was to use cuts to capital gains taxes to unleash untapped entrepreneurial potential. (As historian Macabe Keliher has noted in these pages, Hong Kong has long played a central role in the neoliberal imagination—Milton Friedman, for example, thought the city showed "how the free market really works"—but the social consequences of policies there have been "disastrous.")

Kemp and his fellow enterprise zone enthusiasts introduced over twenty bills in the House and Senate during the 1980s. These bills commonly included reductions to capital gains and business taxes, regulatory relief, and accelerated depreciation. Notably, in a memo to Reagan, Kemp argued that enterprise zones would bolster urban support for the GOP: "I obviously believe that enterprise zones are good public policy. But they are also good politics . . . Enterprise Zones can be a symbol—Ronald Reagan's symbol—of hope that the Republican Party will not concede our nation's poorest communities in its attempt to become the majority party." Reagan was convinced. He asked Congress to help "communities to break the bondage of dependency. Help us to free enterprise by permitting debate and voting 'yes' on our proposal for enterprise zones in America."

Although enterprise zones enjoyed the notable backing of the White House, most Republicans in Congress, and a smattering of Democrats, the federal initiative was stymied by key Democrats in pivotal positions. Among them was Chairman of the House Ways and Means Committee Dan Rostenkowski, who remained unconvinced for most of the 1980s. Nevertheless, enterprise zones proliferated at the state level, propelled by a growing cadre of backers at the Heritage Foundation, the American Legislative Exchange Council, the Cato Institute, and the Sabre Foundation. As Karen Mossberger demonstrates in *The Politics of Ideas and the Spread of Enterprise Zones* (2000), by the end of the decade over forty states had their own enterprise zone programs.

Democratic skepticism wouldn't last in the face of these inroads. By the 1990s Democrats such as Charles Rangel—who had voted against several enterprise zone bills the decade before—introduced their own versions of the idea, and the 1992 Democratic Party platform included a commitment to introduce enterprise zones. Indeed, to the disappointment of those looking for a comprehensive federal response to the inequities highlighted by the Los Angeles uprisings, Bill Clinton called for "new incentives for the private sector, an investment tax credit," and "urban enterprise zones." Democratic support only increased in the late 1980s and early 1990s despite growing signs of the shortcomings of the enterprise zone approach.

Once elected, Clinton directed Vice President Al Gore to develop enterprise proposals for cities. Concerned that the language sounded overly Reaganite, Gore rebranded the Democratic version as "empowerment zones." In keeping with the New Democrats' "third way" approach, the program blended targeted tax incentives—including those designed to encourage the hiring of zone residents, relief from property taxes, and accelerated depreciation—with $1 billion in block grants. At the same time, Clinton was keen to reassure voters that empowerment zones did not signal a return to big government: "this is no Great Society," he intoned. In 1994 nine cities won empowerment zone status—Atlanta, Chicago, New York (which got two zones), Cleveland, Baltimore, Detroit, Philadelphia-Camden, and Los Angeles—and three years later, an additional fifteen urban zones were granted the designation.

In short, the idea of using tax breaks to nudge private investment has been a central instrument of neoliberal governance for decades. As historian Quinn Slobodian notes in his new book, *Crack-Up Capitalism* (2023), the central innovation it marked in urban planning was "the way it short-circuited local government and handed control straight to developers."

THE EVIDENCE regarding the performance of the enterprise and empowerment zone programs is remarkably consistent. It suggests that they were either ineffective in stimulating new economic activity, or, in the rarer cases where new activity can be attributed to zone incentives (as opposed to activity that was likely to have occurred in any case), extraordinarily expensive. In their exhaustive 2002 study of seventy-five enterprise zones in thirteen states, urban planning scholars Alan Peters and Peter Fisher found that the tax incentives had "little or no positive impact" on economic growth. Likewise, in their 2014 book on empowerment zones, Michael Rich and Robert Stoker argued that although "several EZ cities produced improvements in their distressed neighborhoods . . . the gains were modest." They concluded that "none of the local EZ programs fundamentally transformed distressed urban neighborhoods."

In the UK, supporters of enterprise zones highlight the Docklands, which went from a derelict port to a thriving financial services hub. In 1988 Howe returned to the Docklands to laud the transformation. "Ten years ago today," he proclaimed, "we set out together a future vision of economic revival which accepted as its first base the beneficence of the capitalist system. Ten years later the sight we survey exceeds our wildest dreams. The future we saw then is successfully at work today."

Yet the government's own assessment shows that relatively few jobs were created and that each one cost $35,000 to $45,000 in spending and lost revenue. Furthermore, the much-heralded trickle-down effect appears wholly theoretical. The area is still home to some of the most "income deprived households" in the UK. Indeed, Tower Hamlets ranked as the most deprived local authority in London (out of thirty-three such regions) and the 24th most deprived in England as a whole (out of 326) in 2015. As of 2019–20, some 56 percent of children in Tower Hamlets live in income-deprived households—the highest rate in England. By contrast, as of 2023, the average salary of those working in Tower Hamlets is £74,930, while the median household income in 2019 was £30,760—suggesting that financial services workers are largely commuting into the area, and that whatever community wealth *is* being created isn't going to the worstoff. The region's economic transformation has thus exacerbated inequality and delivered little tangible benefit to the poor.

A similar story is unfolding in the United States with OZs. Though Congress and the Treasury have failed to mandate reporting requirements, numerous attempts have been made to get a handle on where the money is going, what kinds of projects are being stimulated, and who benefits. Some patterns can be readily discerned. The congressional Joint Committee on Taxation has found that as of 2020, OZ funds held $48 billion in assets, 86 percent of which is invested in real estate, finance, insurance, and holding companies. Moreover, it estimates that OZs will cost the federal government $8.2 billion in foregone tax revenue for fiscal years 2020–24, with the costliest elements coming due in 2028. All told, it could cost as much as $103 billion after ten years.

Given the scale of the program, Brett Theodos and colleagues at the Urban Institute have argued that "Opportunity Zones is the largest ongoing federal community economic development program" in the United States. But most of this money has gone to a very small percentage of zones: 5 percent of the zones received 78 percent of overall investment; just 1 percent of the zones received nearly half; and half attracted no investment at all by the end of 2020. The law allows 10 percent of OZ funds to be invested outside of the zones, meaning that high-income areas have enjoyed tax-advantaged investment, and as economists at the Treasury's Office of Tax Analysis concluded last November, the kinds of census tracts that have drawn investment have not been the poorest. On the contrary, they tend to be more educated and have higher home values than tracts that have been passed over.

On the questions of who the investors are and what kinds of projects they invest in, the evidence is abundantly clear: they are very wealthy, and they are mostly investing in real estate. Given that 75 percent of capital gains are concentrated in the top 1 percent of households, it is not surprising that that average income of OZ investors in 2019 was over $1 million. These investors, naturally, are looking to maximize returns, which is why the disproportionate flow of OZ investment is going into market-rate rental housing and commercial and industrial real estate. Less than 3 percent is going into operating businesses. As economists Ofer Eldar and Chelsea Garber argued last June, there is a "strong mismatch" between the program's "stated purpose and its actual terms."

Much to the vexation of OZ supporters at EIG and elsewhere, the press has leapt on examples of OZ investments that seem to violate the spirit of a law intended to stimulate new investment and "help the poor." In Portland, Oregon, for example—dubbed Tax Breaklandia by *Bloomberg Business Week*—the state nominated nearly all of the city's central business district for OZ benefits, which meant that investors in projects such as a $600 million development of the downtown Portland Ritz-Carlton will avoid paying capital gains tax. Elsewhere, after his eleven-day stint in the Trump White House, Anthony Scaramucci directed his hedge fund, SkyBridge Capital, to invest in one of Richard Branson's Virgin Hotels in New Orleans's already gentrifying Warehouse District. This area gained OZ status despite having little trouble attracting capital; the hotel project was already in the works before OZs became law but got to take the tax benefit nevertheless.

Baltimore, Maryland, is just one of many similar examples. The Port Covington neighborhood drew particular attention when it was revealed that Maryland's Republican governor and part-time real estate developer, Larry Hogan, revised his nominations to include the tract, despite being told by officials that it did not qualify. The community had relatively few people, was not poor, and was surrounded by mostly high-income tracts, but since a sliver of a parking lot within Port Covington fell within a qualified tract, it gained OZ status after assiduous lobbying efforts on behalf of a project bankrolled by Goldman Sachs's Urban Investment Group and Under Armour founder Kevin Plank. (It was subsequently found that the overlap was actually due to a mapping error, but the tract remained an OZ.) The project, already underway with the aid of state and city tax breaks before designation, aimed to build a hotel, offices, market-rate apartments, and retail aimed at millennials. In the words of urban studies scholar Robert Stoker, Port Covington's designation as an OZ is "a classic example of a windfall benefit."

In his recent book, Wessel scoured the land to identify positive cases—those that did seem to correspond to the spirit of the law and reflect the aims set out by OZ evangelists. He did find some, including the SoLa Impact project that has built genuinely affordable housing in Los Angeles; the Chicago Cook Workforce Partnership, which used QOF capital to construct a new building in which the investors are not charging rent above that needed to cover property taxes; and investment in affordable housing and a local newspaper in Brookville, Indiana. But, as Wessel points out, these kinds of projects "draw fewer OZ dollars than the office towers, condos, and luxury apartments. . . . the OZ money going to heavily celebrated, heart-warming projects appears to be a small percentage of total OZ investments."

In short, enterprise and opportunity zones face six key problems:

1. They reward the wealthy for making investments they would have made anyway.

The aim is to stimulate new investment that would not have occurred without the tax incentives. But the risk—and the reality in the overwhelming proportion of cases—is that tax expenditures go to subsidizing developments that would have happened anyway. As a result, government is wasting potentially vast amounts of money. This pattern is clearly evident for OZs, which led economists Patrick Kennedy and Harrison Wheeler to conclude in April 2021 that OZs "disproportionately benefit a narrow subset of tracts in which economic conditions were already improving prior to implementation of the tax subsidy."

2. They amount to shuffling the decks.

In many cases investors are simply relocating investments that would have happened anyway so that they occur inside a zone. In other cases, designated zone areas are widened so that projects already in the works receive tax benefits. As in Port Covington, lobbyists have sought to persuade governors or the Treasury to add certain census tracts because of planned investments that fall just outside the zone. In one particularly egregious example, Florida's then-governor, Rick Scott, amended his nominations for OZs in order to add a tract in which a donor, Wayne Huizenga Jr., had planned to develop a superyacht arena. In these cases there is no net new investment; money is simply moved around.

3. They pay little attention to who exactly is benefitting.

Even if the tax incentives spark new investment, the distributional consequences are ignored; it's usually the wealthy—not the poor—who are benefitting most, or benefitting at all. The construction of market-rate housing in distressed neighborhoods is more likely to push residents out—or force them to spend even more on rent—than to benefit them. As Kennedy and Wheeler note, "the direct tax incidence of the OZ program is likely to benefit households in the 99th percentile of the national household income distribution." The conceit that these rewards will be shared with low-income earners is just another holdover of trickle-down economics.

4. They risk making things worse for the poor.

Indeed, OZs may even exacerbate inequality. Besides displacement, new investment can trigger gentrification as expensive coffee shops, microbreweries, and boutique clothing stores replace diners, dive bars, and dollar stores. From the point of view of the gentrifier, the neighborhood has improved, but the ordinary resident faces a rising cost of living and a diminished sense of community.

5. The benefits—when they exist—may not be justified by the costs.
Even in cases where zone incentives seem to have a made a difference without fueling displacement and gentrification, the costs associated with foregone tax revenue must be weighed against what could have been done with.

6. They are undemocratic.
With the possible exception of empowerment zones, the zone idea fails to give residents any say as to what kind of investments they want or need. Unlike mechanisms such as participatory budgeting, which empower residents to have a say in the way local government revenue is spent, poor people are excluded from all OZ decision-making processes; the best one can hope for is the good intentions of venture capitalists and state governors. The reality is that most investors are motivated by avoiding taxes and securing profitable returns; whether poor people benefit doesn't factor into their decisions.

FORTUNATELY, there are alternatives.

The first step is to strike at the ideological heart of the matter. In essence, the zone approach is based on the claim that what poor areas need is more capitalism: taxes and regulation are considered fetters on private investment, which is portrayed as the only efficient or valid means for combatting distressed communities. As Butler put it when I interviewed him in 2015, "the capital gains tax argument, which is what Kemp and [Joe] Lieberman and myself were arguing, is the 'risk-taking' argument. In order to help small businesses get access to capital, you have to make it worthwhile for venture capitalists to say, 'I'm prepared to gamble on this and I want my reward from success.'" In reality, unfettered capitalism is to blame; as capital sweeps in and out of neighborhoods, all but the lucky few are left behind. What these communities need is not greater exposure to venture capital but protection from capricious cycles of disinvestment, displacement, and rent-seeking.

Second, rather than focusing on enhancing the *exchange* value of land—which is of little use to non-property holders and of only marginal use to those who own property to live in rather than as an investment vehicle—urban policy should be directed to enhancing the use value of land. In 2019 Senator Ron Wyden of Oregon proposed legislation to prohibit OZ investments in stadiums, self-storage, and luxury apartments, but even if this were to pass into law—a slim chance in today's Congress, especially given the pro-OZ groups that have now mobilized to protect their interests—it likely would not stimulate the kinds of investments needed to materially improve deprived neighborhoods, in part because shareholder primacy leads investors to chase short-term profits.

A more substantial vision for reform was proposed last May by Representative Lloyd Doggett and Senator Sherrod Brown, including a Wyden-like provision prohibiting high-end development as well as a requirement that QOFs include community representation on their boards and "provide meaningful opportunities for community input." But again, the chances that a bill with truly "meaningful" community empowerment would pass is slim, and even if it did, investors would likely judge the resulting program as too saddled with red tape and park their money elsewhere. Moreover, this was precisely the approach taken in empowerment zones, which proved largely unsuccessful. We should look instead to direct state investment in social infrastructure of the sort that legal scholar Richard Schragger urges in his book *City Power: Urban Governance in a Global Age* (2010)—from affordable housing, schools, and good-paying jobs to medical clinics, playgrounds and sports facilities, libraries, and affordable, high-quality public transit.

Third, we must think beyond tax-based redistribution, which otherwise leaves capitalism to its own devices. An alternative strategy is to strike at the heart of capital itself to change the institutional foundations of our political economy and create new forms of ownership and production that put wealth and power in the hands of ordinary citizens. As Joe Guinan and Martin O'Neill argue in *The Case for Community Wealth Building* (2019), local communities can be transformed in ways that benefit and empower the working class through networks of collaborative institutions such as worker cooperatives, community land trusts, and public banks. As the examples of Cleveland, Ohio, and the City of Preston in England demonstrate, this strategy can succeed even in places ravaged by deindustrialization and austerity. Indeed, a 2018 study found that, due in part to its community wealth building strategies, Preston was the mostimproved city in the UK based on several measures including employment, workers' pay, inequality, house prices, transport, and the environment. Urban policy and economic development should be directed to supporting the kinds of transformations that enable cities to recirculate capital *through* the community—rather than *upward* to investors.

In the end, enterprise and opportunity zones are founded on the discredited premise of trickle-down economics. In this, they reflect a failure to learn the lessons of the past. We should bury this zombie idea once and for all. Only then will we be empowered to build a just future for all communities.

MICROFINANCE'S IMAGINED UTOPIA
Kevin P. Donovan

WHEN THE GRAMEEN BANK and the Bangladeshi academic who helped start it, Muhammad Yunus, won the 2006 Nobel Peace Prize, the event cemented the rise of microfinance—the style of global development they pioneered. The prize committee joined supporters such as the U.S. Agency for International Development (USAID) and governments across the Global South in valorizing the idea that making small loans to those typically considered unworthy of credit could "empower" them and "alleviate" poverty.

After experimenting for a number of years, Yunus launched the Grameen Bank in 1983, lending working capital (often as little as a few dollars) to rural women making handicrafts or running shops. Grameen's appeal was captured in the idea of "social business" that Yunus extolled. While he readily critiqued exclusionary banks and predatory money-lenders, microcredit was hardly opposed to commerce. Instead, it made markets the key domain for fighting global poverty. After all, these were loans not handouts. Lenders expected women to use the money profitably, often grouping Grameen borrowers together so they were jointly liable for individual debts. They believed that social pressure and mutual support would significantly diminish the rate of default—and it did.

By the turn of the millennium, Yunus was microcredit's most effective global salesman. The 1997 Microcredit Summit in Washington, D.C., launched a plan "to reach 100 million of the world's poorest families, especially the women of those families, with credit for self-employment." Influential advocates such as Nicholas Kristof and Hillary Clinton spread the gospel through emotional appeals to individuals and institutions: finally, here was something that could lift millions out of poverty. And the message resonated, not least because it aligned with the prevailing liberalism of the time. It was pro-poor and pro-woman, and it hinged on private initiative rather than state welfare or political struggle.

Yet not even half a decade after Yunus's Nobel Prize, the popular consensus on microfinance started to unravel. A series of crises among borrowers suggested that virtuous "credit" could not so easily be divorced from odious "debt." In the Indian state of Andhra Pradesh, a leading laboratory for microfinance, the government's enthusiasm for the program and a turn to profit-oriented lending led to widespread, exploitative loans. Once-negotiable microloan repayment schedules became increasingly stringent and extractive. Some households were borrowing from as many as ten different institutions, often using one expensive loan to pay off another as they struggled with agrarian crises and precarious employment. One government report found at least fifty-four suicides, as lenders harassed borrowers for repayment. These deaths were the most visible signs of a promise gone awry. When local politicians denounced the obligation to pay creditors, millions of citizens refused to repay their outstanding loans. By one account, 98 percent collection rates suddenly dropped to less than 10 percent.

The crisis and backlash in Andhra Pradesh was hardly unique. In her 2010 book *Poverty Capital*, Ananya Roy details how microfinance's uptake in more commercial models eroded any potential virtue in the Grameen Bank model. Some microfinance proponents sounded alarms over disasters such as Andhra Pradesh; even mainstream economists cast doubt on the benefits of microloans. Yet others, such as the World Bank's microfinance evangelists, blamed the problems in places such as Andhra Pradesh less on the extractive nature of debt than on the "populist pronouncements" of politicians, which encouraged "clients to question their obligations to repay." In the face of controversy, advocates rebranded microcredit as "financial inclusion," with digital technologies for credit scoring and payment heralded as new means to reach the promise. By 2015 the global microfinance industry acquired an estimated 200 million clients. Since then, digital lenders have further expanded the frontier, often with devastating effects.

The simultaneous allure and anxiety that characterizes microfinance has spurred two new histories of the industry. The books—Nick Bernards's *A Critical History of Poverty Finance: Colonial Roots and Neoliberal Failures* (2022) and Joanne Meyerowitz's *A War on Global Poverty: The Lost Promise of Redistribution and the Rise of Microcredit* (2021)—depart from the optimism of 1997 and 2006. They instead view microfinance as rooted in colonial and neoliberal models for the governing of workers, the extraction of value, and the maintenance of inequality. Through attention to the ideas and instruments of microfinanciers, these scholars offer important critiques. Yet in attending mostly to the archives of development practitioners, they offer fewer insights into what borrowers want and how they challenge hegemonic finance. Moreover, seeing the history of microfinance as an ongoing repetition of exploitation means the authors cannot offer a vision in which finance—whether socialized, decommodified, or democratized—might play a role in improving the lives of the global majority.

IN INTERNATIONAL DEVELOPMENT, crisis and critique are rarely enough to scrap favored initiatives. As Bernards argues in his new book on "poverty finance," a term he uses to include microfinance and associated initiatives, even sullied ideas can live on despite coming to nothing. Examining microfinance's antecedents as far back as interwar empires, he writes that "Most of these have failed on their own terms; virtually all have failed to deliver substantial benefits; none have unambiguously delivered significant, large-scale reductions in poverty." This history of failure is, ironically, a reason for the continued commitment to microfinance and its variants. Quoting geographer Jamie Peck, Bernards writes that poverty finance tends to "fail and flail forward." A peculiar mix of evergreen optimism, opportunistic forgetting, and capitalist imperatives have conspired repeatedly to rehabilitate poverty capital as a talisman of progress.

In contrast to the promise of "empowerment," microfinance more often resembles "a grimly exploitative mechanism for extraction." In Bernards's assessment, these initiatives transfer responsibility from states onto impoverished workers, especially women, who must labor to keep up with exacting and expensive loans. But Bernards's critique goes deeper: microfinance is built on a "fantasy" that denies its true function as a form of rule rather than assistance. Whether developing insurance products for the unemployed or providing agricultural credit to farmers, the staunch commitment to using financial services to meet public purposes depends on the deferral of success—the continuation of poverty and the lack of developmental progress. Indeed, he argues, when microcredit reached global prominence, it was already part of an unacknowledged, century-long repertoire for managing poverty.

Casting his view back to British and French colonial initiatives, Bernards documents a genealogy of poverty finance. He veers widely across the twentieth century—from money lending in Punjab to West African agricultural exports—to argue that debt was often a means to discipline labor and appropriate commodities cheaply. Colonial merchants profited, in part, through the limitations on credit: being the only lender in town meant trading firms and their brokers could reliably secure the cocoa or palm oil grown in places such as Nigeria or the Gold Coast. By the 1940s some British administrators wanted to expand financial services to boost colonial exports and welfare, yet commercial lenders were often hesitant to take risks or part ways with their capital for long-term investments. Capital, for Bernards, needs to be coaxed outward from its own safe spaces of accumulation, thus colonial developmental ideologies inaugurated an ongoing project by aid organizations and states to convince financiers to lend to poor people across the Global South.

As his history makes clear, finance does not occur in a virtual realm detached from borrowers' everyday activities. A world of gruelling, un-certain work stands between the dispersal of a loan and its repayment. Farmers who borrow to buy seeds and fertilizer are obliged to labor on cash crops. Urban women who take a loan to cover school fees need to produce and sell petty crafts. In this way, poverty finance governs how peasants and workers spend their time. Insofar as it succeeds, it draws people into markets and furthers the imperative to labor. Yet the low and volatile income their labor earns hardly assures success: governments and aid organizations, as Bernards argues, must continually work to create these markets and maintain participation in them. In the colonial era, for example, administrators fretted about a lack of thrift: "The Gold Coast African . . . prefers to spend lavishly, even foolishly, when he has money; and to borrow when he has none," they complained. Colonial officials hoped to instill more commercial mindsets, yet this was expensive and risky. Missionary schools and cooperative agricultural systems tried to encourage new types of financial habits, but the enduring parsimony of the colonial state and the risks of political disputes limited such efforts by French or British officials. For Bernards, forgetting this colonial inheritance allows contemporary financial inclusion efforts—from digital loans to climate insurance—to repeat the extraction and exploitation of the past. Only with an honest appraisal of this history can the presumed novelties of microfinance be fully recognized for what they are.

MEYEROWITZ'S BOOK also belies the notion that microfinance was a radical, new idea in the 1990s. Like Bernards, Meyerowitz argues that redistributive justice was never its goal, but she offers a more recent history of microfinance focused on the 1970s. In her view, this was the decade when market-oriented initiatives came to dominate the aid sector, providing the stage for neoliberal transformations. Meyerowitz draws on recent scholarship, including books by Adom Getachew and Samuel Moyn, that trace the demise of more ambitious programs for remaking national and international economies. In place of an earlier focus on infrastructure, industrial employment, and reformed trade regimes, in the '70s, attention shifted to prioritizing the "basic needs" of the world's poor: food, water, shelter, and schooling. Those commitments edged out alternative visions like the New International Economic Order, which called for redistributing economic power and resources to poor countries. Meyerowitz shows that opposition to muscular redistribution came not only from business interests and their conservative activist allies but from self-identified liberals and leftists as well. Neoliberalism, in this telling, is the result not of Reagan and Thatcher's electoral victories, nor the changing fate of corporate profitability. Rather, it arose from surprising intellectual affinities that discredited social democratic and socialist politics and valorized the expansion of markets to meet public goals. As her subtitle suggests, redistributive politics faded, deferred to a later date that would never arrive. In microfinance small loans stand in for improved terms of trade, developmental states, and welfare programs.

Microfinance also reflects Meyerowitz's second focal point, which is the repositioning of women within international development. While Bernards has surprisingly little to say about how poverty capital came to focus on women in the Global South, Meyerowitz rightly foregrounds the significance of gendered notions of uplift and empowerment in remaking international aid. Prior to the '70s, women were most often cast as "excessive breeders" or unqualified carers who needed training and guidance to limit procreation and improve hygiene. Over the next decade, "development experts repositioned women as producers . . . and made increasing attempts to pull indigent women's labor out of subsistence and into the market economy."

While the economic downturns of the '70s forced women around the world into marketplaces and commodity production, Meyerowitz focuses mostly on the debate in U.S. policy circles over women's role in global development efforts. The notion that "development" bypassed or harmed women came from many quarters; Meyerowitz shows how this gendered approach gained influence as key advocates "downplayed feminism" and instead depicted women as underused economic resources. She draws on the archives of the Ford Foundation and USAID, two funders that promulgated a style of developmentalism that defanged more radical options. Adrienne Germain of the Ford Foundation receives special attention, not least for her interest in Bangladesh and friendship with Yunus. Germain energetically worked to convince male-dominated institutions that poor countries could not "afford to abuse and under-utilize fully half" their people—one of the few resources they had.

Other advocates focused their attention on the U.S. aid apparatus. Liberal feminists delicately maneuvered to mandate that USAID integrate women into development programs in 1973. However, implementation faced a slow road, bogged down by resistance and logistical difficulties. A requirement that year—long before the Reagan revolution—insisted that USAID work through private and voluntary entities as much as possible. Not only were USAID and others increasingly committed to creating markets, that effort had also to be executed through non-state intermediaries. Though government institutions maintained a role—through enabling regulation, funding basic infrastructure, or even serving as a guarantor as USAID did for the Mexican microfinance institution Accion—much of the work was delegated to nonprofit and commercial entities.

Many organizations rushed to take advantage of the new government funding for women's livelihoods. Few exemplify the odd alliances of microfinance as keenly as Women's World Banking, founded—by a Ghanaian entrepreneur, Esther Ocloo; a Gandhian cooperative organizer, Ela Bhatt; and a Wall Street veteran, Michaela Walsh—to "provide guarantees to banks that made microloans to women." Bhatt's Self-Employed Women's Association was something of a model, having helped illiterate women navigate loan applications and then, in 1974, opening its own bank. These unlikely allies were united in their view that women were disproportionately poor and thus uniquely positioned to provide basic needs and better investments than men. The resulting initiative modeled how a style of discreet feminism could be integrated into poverty capitalism.

While the shifts in the 1970s formally prioritized women's well-being and livelihoods, they hardly protected women's rights. Meyerowitz—whose previous work centered on the history of gender and sexuality in the United States—sees a divergence between that context and how microfinance worked internationally. Just as Black women were being recast as undeserving "welfare queens" in the United States, racialized women elsewhere in the world were depicted as the key to development and proper recipients of aid. Yet rather than an irony, these two trends aligned. The movement against welfare was an attack on rights-bearing citizens—a collusion between patriarchs and neoliberals, as Melinda Cooper has shown. And, while international aid organizations called for empowering women, microfinance offered nothing beyond charity and the market. By locking women into philanthropy and commerce, it undermined an already tenuous hold on rights-based claims-making by female citizens. In both movements, women's well-being was pursued through paternalistic oversight and market involvement.

BOTH BERNARDS AND MEYEROWITZ critically examine development discourse, their books tracking development practitioners and scholars—those credentialed "experts" who move easily between World Bank conclaves, Ford Foundation workshops, and Euro-American university seminars. These experts wrote voluminously, and their reports and archives tell an important version of development history. Yet Bernards's and Meyerowitz's sources only rarely capture details about the people who aid organizations claim to serve. The livelihoods and aspirations of the people affected by poverty capital recede in these histories. The trouble with this double erasure—first by development elites, second by historians—is that it only produces creditor histories. Borrowers become an undifferentiated population of poor victims. For Meyerowitz and Bernards, borrowers exist principally in what we might call *the indigent slot*, with a nod to the anthropologist Michel-Rolph Trouillot's concept of "the savage slot." For Trouillot anthropology was complicit in a Western project of distorting and containing colonized people through the framework of "native" or "primitive." Relying on sources that see people through the lens of indigence, need, and suffering, historians may be rightly critical of development experts and their projects, but they cannot sufficiently account for the "the poor," their differences, and their ambitions.

The elision of popular economic practices in these histories also stands in contrast to the microfinance institutions they analyze. Proponents of poverty capital have a longstanding interest in the everyday habits and behaviors of ordinary people. Indeed, the industry often invested in research on the lives and livelihoods of workers and peasants as part of their effort to extend debt to them. Large household surveys might ask how much people can afford to repay; behavioral economists might try to discern how finance intersects with other obligations. As Julia Elyachar writes, the animating idea of this style of developmentalism has been "to reconstitute the social networks and cultural practices of the poor as part of the free market." In Cairo, where she studied, this involved mapping and appropriating the talents, proclivities, and friendships of would-be borrowers. In other words, the practices of people lumped together as "indigent" hold the attention of the microfinance industry because the sector rises or falls on the diversity of borrowers' livelihoods, cultures, and ambitions.

One effect of the narrative imbalance between creditors and borrowers is to suggest that microfinance elites are uniquely responsible for the shape of poverty capital. Bernards gives the impression that austere colonial administrators and risk-adverse European bankers alone were responsible for the uneven extent of financial services. But in many cases, it was not so much European greed and neglect nor an abstract logic of capitalism that foreclosed access to financial services. Instead, the choices of colonized people not to borrow money or save it in a bank was (and remains) an important strategy to maintain autonomy, a deliberate distancing from capitalist extraction. Their refusal is also evidence of what Parker Shipton calls competing "fiduciary cultures," the normative ideas that shape how people give and receive, trust and repay. As he shows in a trilogy of books, the Luo people in Kenya tactically and opportunistically engage with state and commercial finance. They often refuse to partake because bank loans are at odds with their own moral, sacred, and economic commitments—most notably a strong preference against commodifying and mortgaging land. Convincing Luo people and many others to become borrowers, savers, or contributors to insurance schemes requires accommodating—or changing—their ideas about worth, risk, and allegiance. Financial exclusion is not merely something done *to* people; exclusion can be a moral and political position taken *by* people.

The critical focus on development experts also downplays the fact that many borrowers are eager financial actors. Historically many people debarred from banks have demanded access to financial services. While their voices are not necessarily found in the archives of USAID or the World Bank, they are accessible to historians. Many of the protests that challenged colonial rule in the 1940s and '50s included demands for better access to agricultural credit. For instance, in 1948 the prominent Ugandan activist Ignatius Musazi and his supporters called for wide-ranging reforms, including the establishment of an agricultural bank that would finance African production. When the Uganda Credit & Savings Bank opened its doors to African borrowers a few years later, there was a rush for loan applications. Applicants were usually relatively well-off men, with control of fertile land and a hand in local government, but less well-to-do aspirants also saw this instance of poverty capital as a necessary instrument for their own advancement. In the coming years they continued to advocate for an expansion of financial services, meaningfully remaking and challenging elite programs.

Today's critics of poverty capital must come to terms with the reasons people desire credit, and this demands attention to particular fiduciary cultures and shifting ethics. Debtors cannot be defined solely as victims of circumstance. Understanding borrowers' worlds and how they have pursued, challenged, or accommodated poverty capital is a necessary part of the history of microfinance, and it is critical to reduce poverty and transform finance.

Anthropologists have more successfully wrestled with microfinance as something that people might turn to for their own purposes, not only as victims of aggressive lending or dire need. Their work offers less political clarity—since not every loan is a Faustian bargain—but it better explains why poverty capital has the reach it does. Juli Huang, for instance, lived with Bangladeshi women who took out loans to work as "iAgents," information brokers with smartphones and tablets. In navigating the move out of their homes to market-mediated livelihoods, these women struggled not only to repay their debts but to maintain their standing within the community. But it wasn't all coercive pressure; they were also drawn to new opportunities. In Huang's approach, women's lives are not merely shaped by poverty nor are they reduced to subjects of neoliberalism. Rather, they are pulled in multiple, sometimes competing directions, making do in situations characterized by ambiguity. At once daughters and wives, traveling salespersons, and

NGO representatives, they face competing expectations and respond through the "strategic juggling of multiple, simultaneous, and often conflicting" actions.

Research like Huang's exposes the limits of the "indigent slot" in understanding the continued popularity of microfinance. The ambiguous lack of clarity for borrowers and regulators alike gives microfinance some of its enduring power. Indeed, many come to microfinance for reasons other than borrowing. The sector has become an enormous employer, providing a path to income and respectability. In Sohini Kar's ethnography of microfinance in Kolkata, the work of loan officers is not only revealed as grueling, but also risky, as officers face "stigmatization as debt collectors." Yet working for a microfinance institution also offers a paycheck and the promise of advancement for marginalized Indians. As a result, many agree to undertake the labor necessary to further financialization.

In her compelling new book, *Making Women Pay* (2022), Smitha Radhakrishnan further explores the diverse motivations that sustain poverty capital. She tells the story of a woman she calls Shankari, who formed or led twelve microfinance groups of up to thirty women in her Bengaluru neighborhood. This work was part of a broader effort through which Shankari "[advocated] for her neighborhood." Brokering public and private programs not only helped her neighbors, it also made her into a community leader with access to resources. For lenders, women like Shankari are necessary intermediaries, providing branch offices with the social infrastructure and local knowledge to enroll and manage clients. The overlapping interests of brokers like Shankari and microfinance institutions help propel the reach of poverty capital—no less than USAID funds or World Bank reports.

None of this denies the lack of alternatives borrowers face under state austerity, underemployment, and agrarian crisis, nor what Radhakrishnan calls the "gendered value extraction" by microfinance. Organizations such as Grameen focused on women for many reasons, but it was no accident that they could, as Lamia Karim put it, compel women to repay their debts by instrumentalizing the "rural codes of honor and shame" imposed on women. For borrowers, microloans are expensive, with interest rates two to three times more than what banks offer, despite reliable repayment histories. The value women produce is funnelled upwards, through channels characterized by gender, caste, and class inequalities. Within Indian microfinance, Brahmin men dominate the upper echelons of the sectors while women—like Shankari—are relegated to less visible and powerful roles. Patriarchal cultures within the sector militate against female advancement, even while the sector extols its promising vision for women.

BOTH MEYEROWITZ AND BERNARDS are reluctant to advance programs from their histories, but their closing pages do offer hints. Meyerowitz agrees with activists' proposals for international taxation on large firms and polluters, the regulation of multinational corporations, protections for workers, a universal basic income, and debt cancellation for poorer nations. None of these involve microfinance industry practices, and only the last touches on debt directly. Bernards, too, sees little to rehabilitate or reform in microfinance. Instead, he believes lending should be replaced by "democratising control over the global economy," greater redistribution, and the "social provision of basic needs" in housing, food, water, and care.

These are fine goals, but they stand at a distance from the particularities of people's lives, ethics, and aspirations. They are also remote from the workings of the financial sector—micro or otherwise. This is a shame, because it is unwise to cede the levers of finance to international institutions, neoliberal governments, and their banker allies. We need alternatives. Even public provisioning and social democracy rely on monetary mechanisms and financial engineering. A better approach would attend more closely to the specific technical and legal constitution of poverty capital, including its relationship with "mainstream" finance.

A recent collection edited by Fred Block and Robert Hockett offers one potential model. *Democratizing Finance* (2022) is the latest intervention in the Real Utopias Project inaugurated by the late sociologist Erik Olin Wright. Like the other books in the series, this volume focuses on reforms that the editors deem realistic while also possessing the power to meaningfully tame, or even dismantle, capitalism.

The two chapters by the coeditors anchor the book with an intellectual and institutional framework for what Hockett calls "socially useful and maximally inclusive productive enterprise." In contrast to unaccountable and wasteful commercial investment strategies, their reformed financial sector would allocate capital to necessary tasks—for example, a green transition or maintaining a stable supply of important goods—while also reducing inequality and extractive practices. This is a task best undertaken through public administration, not the private bankers who today pursue shareholder profit over collective need. Yet overturning this status quo is difficult, not least because citizens and policymakers operate with a mystified theory of how finance works.

In this mistaken theory, banks serve as intermediaries between the savings they collect and the loans they issue—they first accumulate money through deposits and then lend it out as credit. Instead, Hockett argues that financiers "generate" credit by issuing loans. "Loans make deposits," not the other way around. But only some institutions are legally authorized to generate money through lending. Through state licensing—ultimately shored up by the "full faith and credit of the sovereign"—banks lend funds that can circulate publicly as dollar bills. U.S. banks are thus mere "franchisees" of the Federal Reserve and the Department of Treasury, their powers of credit creation delegated by "we the people."

For Hockett, only a proper theory of finance can help authorize a more accountable use of the state's financial power. This starts with recognizing that public power does already underwrite the financial sector, but it does so to the benefit of private profit rather than collective purpose. A central bank, he argues, is not merely a lender of last resort, able to provide liquidity or other assistance in momentary crisis. The state guarantees private banking even in "ordinary" times. He writes that "We the public sit at the center of the financial system, and generate the resource that circulates through that system—our own monetized full faith and credit." Yet because a mistaken view of banking denies the centrality of public authority of private capital, the latter runs roughshod over the former.

Such a view has far-reaching implications. Hockett and Block propose a series of new public institutions designed to invest—on their own or with non-state entities—in national development. Looking across credit unions, state banks, and beyond, Block calls for reforms such as matching grants and loan guarantees that might conjure a more just allocation of capital. Whether the goal is windmill farms or affordable housing, the state should consider expanding who it allows to become a financial franchisee. It should license public sector agencies and nonprofit organizations to create credit for democratically chosen purposes.

Their envisioned investments focus on large-scale infrastructure, but Block does echo Yunus in arguing that the higher cost of credit for lower-income borrowers should be reduced to support "small-scale entrepreneurial efforts." Hockett likewise supports a push for what microfinanciers now call "financial inclusion." He worries that profit-oriented banks exploit and exclude citizens from the banking system, and he proposes the Federal Reserve provide the infrastructure for digital "wallets" through which ordinary people and firms could make transactions. A public banking infrastructure would outcompete the "payday lenders, check cashers, and other species of 'loan shark,'" he writes in an observation akin to Yunus's condemnation of the "village moneylender." A public bank account would also provide the state a means to channel resources with a greater degree of granularity than currently possible. ("QE for the people," he offers in another catchy slogan.)

Scholars of poverty finance should take note especially of the ideas about public financial infrastructures, more accountable investment decisions, and changes to credit scoring methods. A similar set of imaginative explorations should be undertaken to consider how the specifics of livelihoods, aspirations, and needs may be improved through the public coordination of investment. Critics of microfinance in the Global South would do well to demand not the end of finance *tout court*—such a position is unlikely to be heard anytime soon—but rather a radical transformation of credit, savings, and insurance.

In other ways, though, the Block and Hockett volume is limited by the overwhelming focus on the United States. This methodological nationalism has various shortcomings. For one, when they echo microfinance talking points, they do less to take on the critical insights from the Global South discussed above. Moreover, the international monetary hierarchy where the United States sits at the pinnacle recedes from view. The monetary autonomy of poorer countries is severely limited, as Ndongo Samba Sylla and others have emphasized; so, too, is the capacity of the bureaucracies that would need to administer public investment and financial infrastructures.

Democratic control of finance in the United States or Europe will need to account for these contexts, not least because finance is not confined to one jurisdiction. As the recent monetary tightening by the Federal Reserve and resulting debt stress around the world make clear, what happens at the Fed doesn't stay in the United States. Any real utopia of finance will require an internationalist approach, potentially reducing the capital allocated to the already overdeveloped United States. This project requires tacking back and forth between very different histories and economic contexts. Finance can only be transformed if it puts precarious workers and central bankers in the same frame.

CONTRIBUTORS

Kevin P. Donovan is Lecturer in the Centre of African Studies at the University of Edinburgh.

Claude Fischer is Distinguished Professor of the Graduate School in Sociology at the University of California, Berkeley. His books include *Inequality by Design: Cracking the Bell Curve Myth*.

Leah Gordon is Associate Professor of Education at Brandeis University and author of *From Power to Prejudice: The Rise of Racial Individualism in Midcentury America*. She is working on a book called *Imagining Opportunity: Education and Equality in Modern America*.

Jo Guldi is Professor of History at Southern Methodist University. Her most recent book is *The Long Land War: The Global Struggle for Occupancy Rights*.

Ravi Kanbur is T. H. Lee Professor of World Affairs, International Professor of Applied Economics and Management, and Professor of Economics at Cornell University. He previously worked for the World Bank and led the Human Development and Capability Association.

Lane Kenworthy is Professor of Sociology and Yankelovich Chair in Social Thought at the University of California, San Diego. His most recent books are *Social Democratic Capitalism* and *Would Democratic Socialism Be Better?*.

Martin O'Neill is Professor of Political Philosophy at the University of York. He is coauthor, with Joe Guinan, of *The Case for Community Wealth Building*.

Christopher Newfield is Distinguished Professor of English Emeritus at the University of California, Santa Barbara and Director of Research at the Independent Social Research Foundation in London. His most recent book is *The Great Mistake: How We Wrecked Public Universities and How We Can Fix Them*.

William M. Paris is Assistant Professor of Philosophy at the University of Toronto and a host of the "What's Left of Philosophy?" podcast. He is working on a book called *Racial Justice and Forms of Life: Toward a Critical Theory of Utopia*.

Anne Phillips is Professor Emerita in the Department of Government at the London School of Economics. Her latest book is *Unconditional Equals*.

John Roemer is Elizabeth S. and A. Varick Stout Professor of Political Science and Economics at Yale University. His many books include *Equality of Opportunity* and *Theories of Distributive Justice*.

Gina Schouten is Professor of Philosophy at Harvard University. She is author of *Liberalism, Neutrality, and the Gendered Division of Labor*, and is completing a book called *The Anatomy of Justice: Liberal Egalitarianism for Liberals and Critics Alike*.

Zofia Stemplowska is Professor of Political Theory and Asa Briggs Fellow at Worcester College at the University of Oxford. She is coeditor, with Carl Knight, of *Responsibility and Distributive Justice*.

Christine Sypnowich is Professor and Head of Philosophy at Queen's University in Kingston, Ontario. She is author of *Equality Renewed: Justice, Human Flourishing, and the Egalitarian Ideal* and *The Concept of Socialist Law* and is completing a book on the philosophy of G. A. Cohen.

Nicholas Vrousalis is Associate Professor of Practical Philosophy at Erasmus University Rotterdam. His latest book is *Exploitation as Domination: What Makes Capitalism Unjust*.

Timothy Weaver is Associate Professor of Political Science at the University at Albany (SUNY). He is author of *Blazing the Neoliberal Trail: Urban Political Development in the United States and the United Kingdom*.